Learn to Sell Anything, to Anyone, Anytime Quickly!

Chapter 1:

The Art of Selling: More Than Just a Transaction

Introduction to the fundamental concepts of selling as an art form that involves psychology, sociology, and skillful communication.

Chapter 2:

Understanding Your Product Inside Out

Why product knowledge is power and how to become an expert on what you're selling.

Chapter 3:

Knowing Your Audience: The Key to Persuasion

The importance of understanding customer needs, desires, and pain points.

Chapter 4:

Crafting Your Value Proposition

How to create a compelling value proposition that resonates with customers.

Chapter 5:

The Psychology Behind a Sale

An introduction to the psychological triggers and cues that lead to a purchase decision.

Chapter 6:

Building Rapport and Trust Quickly

Techniques for creating a connection with potential customers from the first interaction.

Chapter 7:

Mastering the Art of Communication

How to listen actively and speak persuasively in any sales situation.

Chapter 8:

The Power of Storytelling in Sales

Using narrative to engage customers and make your product memorable.

Chapter 9:

Overcoming Objections Gracefully

Strategies for addressing and alleviating customer concerns without confrontation.

Chapter 10:

The Strategic Sales Process

An overview of the steps involved in a strategic sales process from prospecting to closing.

Chapter 11:

Prospecting: Finding the Right Customers

How to identify and target individuals who are most likely to buy what you're selling.

Chapter 12:

The First Impression: Opening the Conversation

Tips for making a strong, positive first impression.

Chapter 13:

Qualifying Leads: Is This a Potential Sale?

Methods for determining whether a prospect is a good fit for your product.

Chapter 14:

Presenting Like a Pro Crafting and delivering a presentation that captivates and convinces.

Chapter 15:

Handling Sales Meetings with Confidence

Managing in-person interactions to move the sale forward.

Chapter 16:

The Art of Following Up

When and how to follow up with potential customers to keep the deal alive.

Chapter 17:

Closing Techniques That Work

A guide to various closing techniques and when to use them.

Chapter 18:

The Digital Sales Landscape

Understanding online sales channels and how to leverage them effectively.

Chapter 19:

Social Selling Mastery

Using social media platforms to connect with customers and drive sales.

Chapter 20:

Email Prospecting: Writing Emails That Get Responses

Crafting emails that stand out in a crowded inbox and prompt action.

Chapter 21:

Negotiating Win-Win Solutions

Techniques for negotiations that satisfy both seller and buyer.

Chapter 22:

Sales Metrics and KPIs

Understanding and tracking the key metrics that signal sales performance.

Chapter 23:

Using CRM Systems for Sales Success

Leveraging Customer Relationship Management tools to

enhance sales productivity.

Chapter 24:

Time Management for Sales Professionals

How to prioritize and manage your time for maximum sales efficiency.

Chapter 25:

Building and Managing a Sales Team

Strategies for recruiting, training, and leading a top-performing sales team.

Chapter 26:

Scaling Sales Operations

Expanding your sales operations while maintaining quality and customer service.

Chapter 27:

The Ethics of Selling

Maintaining integrity and ethical practices in your sales approach.

Chapter 28:

Continuous Learning and Adaptation

Staying current in an ever-evolving sales landscape.

Chapter 29:

Leveraging Feedback and Criticism

How to use customer and peer feedback to improve your sales process.

Chapter 30:
Networking and Building Industry Relationships

The role of networking in creating opportunities and boosting sales.

Chapter 31:
Personal Branding for Sales Professionals

Establishing yourself as a thought leader and trusted advisor in your field.

Chapter 32:
Innovation in Sales Techniques

How to stay ahead of the curve with innovative sales techniques and strategies.

Chapter 33:
Conquering Sales Slumps

Dealing with the inevitable ebb and flow of sales performance.

Chapter 34:
The Role of Emotion in Selling

Understanding the emotional journey of the buyer and using it to your advantage.

Chapter 35:

Cross-cultural and Global Selling

Navigating sales across different cultures and international markets.

Chapter 36:
Advanced Persuasion Techniques

Exploring deeper psychological techniques to enhance persuasion skills.

Chapter 37:
Future-proofing Your Sales Career

How to anticipate changes in the market and adjust your sales approach accordingly.

Chapter 38:
Harnessing Technology in Sales

Embracing new technologies that can augment and streamline the sales process.

Chapter 39:
Health and Well-Being for Sales

Chapter 1:

The Art of Selling: More Than Just a Transaction

Selling, at its core, is an ancient art form; it's the tapestry of human desire interwoven with the skill of persuasion. It's both a science and a finesse – not merely a transaction but a symphony of interactions that, when played well, lead to a crescendo of success for both the seller and the buyer.

In the bustling markets of ancient Athens, merchants understood that to sell their wares, they needed more than just a loud voice and a good product; they required an understanding of their buyer's lives, needs, and the subtle art of persuasion. This ancient understanding still rings true today; to excel in sales is to master the delicate balance between knowledge and emotional intelligence.

Real-Life Anecdotes: The Story of a Tech Titan

Take, for instance, the tale of Steve Jobs. Known for his captivating product presentations, Jobs did more than sell technology; he sold an experience, a dream. When unveiling the first iPhone in 2007, he didn't simply list specifications; he crafted a narrative, telling a story of revolution and personal empowerment. He understood his audience's desires for simplicity and elegance in a technologically complex world and presented the iPhone as the magic wand to achieve this.

The Strategy of Storytelling

Following Jobs's lead, our first actionable strategy is storytelling. Begin each day by writing a short story that relates to the product you're selling. How has it transformed a difficulty into a convenience? How has it turned an ordinary moment into an extraordinary one? This daily task will not only improve your communication skills but also arm you with a quiver of compelling stories for your next sales pitch.

Training Program: Understanding the Buyer

The best sales training programs emphasize deep understanding of the buyer's persona. For one week, focus on asking questions rather than pitching your product. Inquire about your customers' challenges, interests, and desires. This exercise will help you grasp the nuances of your customers' needs and sharpen your ability to tailor your pitch accordingly.

Daily Tasks and Training

1. **Morning Reflection:** Start each day by considering the needs and wants of your ideal customer. Who are they? What do they value?

2. **Active Listening Practice:** Engage in at least two conversations daily where your goal is purely to understand the other person's perspective.

3. **Pitch Perfecting:** Allocate 30 minutes to refine your sales pitch, integrating stories and emphasizing how

your product addresses specific customer needs.

4. **Role Play:** End the day with a role-playing exercise, either with a colleague or alone. Simulate a sales scenario and practice overcoming objections.

Actionable Strategies: Building Trust

Building trust is paramount. Always remember, people buy from people, not companies. Trust is cultivated through consistency, expertise, and empathy. Show up consistently on platforms where your customers are active – this could be LinkedIn, a weekly blog, or community events. Share your knowledge without always pitching a sale, and when you engage with customers, do so with the aim of helping, not just selling.

Food for Thought: The Consultative Seller

Consider shifting from being a product pusher to a consultative seller. This approach involves a deep dive into the buyer's context and providing solutions that may even extend beyond the product itself. It is about being a trusted advisor rather than a transactional seller.

Summaries: The Essence of Chapter One

To encapsulate, selling is an intricate art that transcends the mere act of exchanging goods and services for money. It is about:

- **Crafting Stories**: Weaving narratives that resonate with the buyer's aspirations.

- **Understanding Deeply**: Diving into the buyer's world to tailor solutions that feel personal and relevant.

- **Building Trust**: Establishing a consistent, empathetic, and knowledgeable presence.

- **Providing Solutions**: Adopting a consultative

approach that positions you as a trusted advisor.

In each interaction, remember that you're not just aiming for a sale, but for a relationship that could yield a lifetime of sales. This philosophy transforms selling from a mundane task to an art form that enriches both the seller and the buyer, ultimately making the act of selling a rewarding and fulfilling experience.

This chapter sets the stage for a journey into the world of selling, not just as a means to an end but as a path to understanding human needs and fulfilling them with grace, integrity, and effectiveness. As you incorporate these strategies and tasks into your daily routine, remember that every great seller is also a great student – of their product, their customer, and the timeless art of persuasion.

Homework:

1. Identify a product you love and write a brief story about how it impacted your life.

2. Start a journal of customer interactions, noting what works and what doesn't in your communication.

3. Practice the "two ears, one mouth" rule: listen twice as much as you talk in your next sales conversation.

Further Reading:

- "How to Win Friends and Influence People" by Dale Carnegie for mastering human relations.

- "Influence: The Psychology of Persuasion" by Robert B. Cialdini for deep insights into the psychology behind why people say "yes."

- Steve Jobs's iPhone presentation (2007) for a real-life demonstration of storytelling in sales.

Chapter 2:

Understanding Your Product Inside Out

To sell effectively, one must not only know their product but believe in it. Understanding your product inside out is the cornerstone of any successful sales strategy. It instills confidence, enables one to answer questions on the fly, and, most importantly, helps tailor the product's features to the customer's needs.

Real-Life Anecdote: The Mastery of Milton Hershey

Milton Hershey, the founder of The Hershey Chocolate Company, didn't just sell chocolate; he sold the concept of accessible luxury. Hershey's journey began with failure as he started three candy companies that did not succeed. Nevertheless, his perseverance led him to build one of the largest chocolate manufacturers in the world. He achieved this by knowing every aspect of his product and the process of making it – from the farms that provided the milk to the precise method of refining the chocolate. His deep product knowledge enabled him to innovate, leading to the creation of the Hershey's Kiss in 1907, a product that became an icon.

The Need for Comprehensive Knowledge

Taking inspiration from Hershey, let's consider the actionable strategy of daily learning. Each day, take a component of your product and learn everything you can about it. This could be a material it's made from, a feature it offers, or even the story behind its inception. By the end of the week, you will have expanded your product knowledge significantly, enhancing your ability to discuss it authoritatively with customers.

Training Program: Product Immersion

To sell a product well, one must become its student. A comprehensive training program should include:

1. **Product Use**: Use your product daily to understand its functionality and quirks.

2. **Feature Breakdown**: Break down each feature of the product and understand the value it provides.

3. **Competitor Comparison**: Regularly compare your product to its competitors, identifying strengths and weaknesses.

4. **Feedback Loop**: Use customer feedback to gain insight into how the product is used and perceived in the real world.

Daily Tasks and Training

1. **Hands-On Experience**: Start every morning using the product, familiarizing yourself with its nuances.

2. **Feature Focus**: Each day, pick a single feature to learn

about deeply. How does it work? Why is it valuable?

3. **Competitive Analysis**: Once a week, study a competitor's product to sharpen your understanding of your product's unique selling proposition (USP).

4. **Market Trends**: End the day reviewing industry news and trends that may affect your product's relevance.

Actionable Strategies: The Consultative Approach

Become a consultant rather than just a salesperson. Help your customers understand not just what your product does but how it fits into their lives or businesses. This consultative approach requires a deep understanding of your product's ecosystem – the problems it solves, the benefits it offers, and the kind of support customers can expect.

Food for Thought: The Ingredient Behind Success

Why do customers choose one product over another? Often, it is not the product itself but the story and conviction behind it. Your product knowledge can imbue your sales pitch with the passion that convinces customers they're not just buying a product – they're investing in a solution.

Summary: Becoming the Product Expert

The second chapter reinforces the importance of product expertise in the art of selling:

- **Product Usage**: Becoming an everyday user to appreciate the product's value and quirks.

- **Feature Familiarity**: Understanding each feature's purpose and benefits to answer any query with confidence.

- **Competitor Awareness**: Knowing your competitors as

well as you know yourself to articulate your product's uniqueness effectively.

- **Customer Feedback**: Using real-world insights to refine your pitch and understand your product's impact.

- **Market Savviness**: Staying abreast of market trends to position your product proactively.

Homework:

1. Create a "Product Bible" – a comprehensive guide detailing every aspect of your product.

2. Role-play challenging questions about your product with a colleague and provide feedback to each other.

3. Write a blog post or social media content piece that showcases a unique aspect of your product.

Further Reading:

- "Product Knowledge Mastery" – a fictional book for further understanding of how to know a product inside out.

- "The Innovator's Dilemma" by Clayton M. Christensen for insights into how product knowledge can lead to innovation.

- The story of Milton Hershey for motivation on the importance of product knowledge in building a brand.

By the end of this chapter, you are not just familiar with your product; you are its champion. Your knowledge is both broad and deep, allowing you to sell with the conviction and authenticity that resonates with buyers and turns them into lifelong customers.

Chapter 3:

Knowing Your Audience:
The Key to Persuasion

In any form of communication, understanding your audience is the most critical element. In sales, it's the cornerstone upon which all persuasive efforts are built. This chapter will delve into the strategies and skills necessary to not just understand your audience, but to empathize with them, tailor your approach to their needs, and, ultimately, to sell to them effectively.

Real-Life Anecdote: The Empathy of Oprah Winfrey

Oprah Winfrey, a media mogul and philanthropist, exemplifies the power of knowing your audience. Her ability to connect with her viewers was uncanny. She did not just host a talk show; she created a platform where people felt seen and heard. Oprah's success hinged on her deep understanding of her audience's emotional landscape. She knew their struggles, aspirations, and the kind of conversation that would resonate with them.

Understanding Before Persuading

Before you can persuade anyone, you must understand them. Your daily task is to research and document the demographics and psychographics of your target market. Spend an hour each day learning about their age, gender, income level, education, hobbies, values, and fears. This knowledge will arm you with the power to tailor your sales message so precisely that it will feel personally crafted for each member of your audience.

Training Program: Audience Analysis

A systematic training program can transform a salesperson from a generalist to a specialist in their audience. This program should consist of:

1. **Market Research**: Use available data to study market trends and customer behavior.

2. **Persona Development**: Create detailed buyer personas that reflect the various segments of your audience.

3. **Empathy Exercises**: Role-play exercises where you put yourself in the customer's shoes.

4. **Feedback Sessions**: Regularly solicit feedback from actual customers to refine your understanding.

Daily Tasks and Training

1. **Research Ritual**: Begin each day with research on one customer segment.

2. **Interaction Insights**: Record and analyze your daily interactions with customers, noting their concerns and feedback.

3. **Persona Practice**: Focus on one buyer persona per day and devise a pitch specifically for that persona.

4. **Empathy Mapping**: At the end of the day, map out the emotional journey a customer goes through when

deciding to purchase your product.

Actionable Strategies: Tailoring the Message

Now, armed with comprehensive knowledge about your audience, begin to tailor your message. Here's how:

- **Use their language**: Speak in a way that resonates with your audience's cultural and social norms.
- **Address their pain points**: Highlight how your product specifically solves problems they face.
- **Align with their values**: Show how your product aligns with what they care about.

Food for Thought: The Authentic Connection

Consider this – people are more likely to buy from someone who genuinely understands them. Authentic connection leads to trust, and trust leads to sales. How can you deepen the connection with your audience to foster this trust?

Summary: Audience Mastery

This chapter stresses the vital role of audience knowledge in sales:

- **Deep Research**: Understanding who your audience is on a granular level.
- **Persona Development**: Crafting detailed profiles that represent segments of your market.
- **Empathy Building**: Developing a sincere empathy for your customers' experiences and emotions.
- **Message Customization**: Tailoring your sales pitch to resonate on a personal level.

By investing time in knowing your audience, you're not just a salesperson; you become a trusted confidant and advisor.

Homework:

1. Create a detailed buyer persona for your primary customer segment.
2. Conduct a survey or interview with actual customers to validate and refine your personas.
3. Draft a customized sales message for each persona, focusing on their unique needs and desires.

Further Reading:

- "Influence: The Psychology of Persuasion" by Robert B. Cialdini to understand the principles that govern human behavior in decision-making.
- "Talking to Strangers" by Malcolm Gladwell for insights on how our interpretations of strangers can be improved.

By mastering the knowledge of your audience, you can make every sale feel like a personal recommendation, enhancing the effectiveness of your pitch and increasing the likelihood of a positive response. This understanding is what transforms a simple transaction into a long-term relationship.

Chapter 4:

Crafting Your Value Proposition

Your value proposition is your promise to the customer. It's the reason they should buy from you and not the competition. Crafting a compelling value proposition is an art that requires a deep understanding of your product's strengths, your customer's needs, and the market landscape.

Real-Life Anecdote: The Precision of Elon Musk

Elon Musk, with his ventures, provides a master class in defining value propositions. Take Tesla, for example. Musk did not simply sell cars; he sold a vision of the future—clean, efficient, and technologically superior. He understood that his value proposition lay not in the vehicle itself but in the innovation, sustainability, and status that owning a Tesla represented.

The Essence of a Strong Value Proposition

To craft your value proposition, begin by identifying the core benefits your product offers. What does it do better than anything else on the market? Why should someone invest their hard-earned money in what you're selling? This is a daily exploration. Each day, identify a feature of your product and convert it into a benefit.

Training Program: Value Proposition Development

To systematically develop a value proposition, your training program should encompass:

1. **Benefit Analysis**: Break down each feature of your product into the benefits it offers.

2. **Market Research**: Understand the market and identify gaps that your product fills.

3. **Customer Validation**: Regularly gather feedback from customers to ensure your value proposition aligns with their perceptions and needs.

4. **Pitch Refinement**: Continuously refine your pitch based on feedback and market changes.

Daily Tasks and Training

1. **Feature-to-Benefit Conversion**: Take one product feature each day and elaborate on its benefits.

2. **Competitive Analysis**: Weekly, study a competitor's value proposition and distinguish your own.

3. **Customer Interviews**: Conduct interviews or surveys to validate the benefits you've identified.

4. **Elevator Pitch Practice**: Daily, practice a 30-second pitch that summarizes your value proposition.

Actionable Strategies: Conveying the Promise

- **Clarity**: Ensure that your value proposition is easy to understand. Avoid jargon and complex language.

- **Relevance**: Tailor your value proposition to address the specific needs and desires of your target audience.
- **Differentiation**: Clearly articulate what makes your product different and better than alternatives.

Food for Thought: The Unique Solution

In a world with endless choices, why should customers choose you? Your value proposition should not just reflect a unique offering, but it should also touch upon the emotional appeal that will resonate with your audience.

Summary: The Art of the Value Proposition

This chapter provides a blueprint for crafting a value proposition that resonates:

- **Benefit-Centric**: Focus on the benefits, not just the features, of your product.
- **Customer-Aligned**: Ensure your value proposition speaks directly to your customer's needs and desires.
- **Market-Aware**: Keep a keen eye on market trends to ensure your proposition stays relevant and competitive.
- **Continuously Refined**: Regularly update your value proposition to reflect new insights and feedback.

Homework:

1. Develop a concise value proposition statement for your product.
2. Create a comparison chart that outlines how your product's benefits stack up against the competition.

3. Refine your value proposition by incorporating feedback from at least ten potential customers.

Further Reading:

- "Value Proposition Design" by Alexander Osterwalder, which offers a practical framework for creating value propositions that sell.
- "Made to Stick" by Chip and Dan Heath, which delves into why some ideas survive and others die, and how this applies to value propositions.

By the end of this chapter, your value proposition should not just be a statement about your product—it should be a declaration of the unique value you bring to every customer interaction. It should capture the essence of what you offer and why it matters, forming the heart of every sales conversation you have.

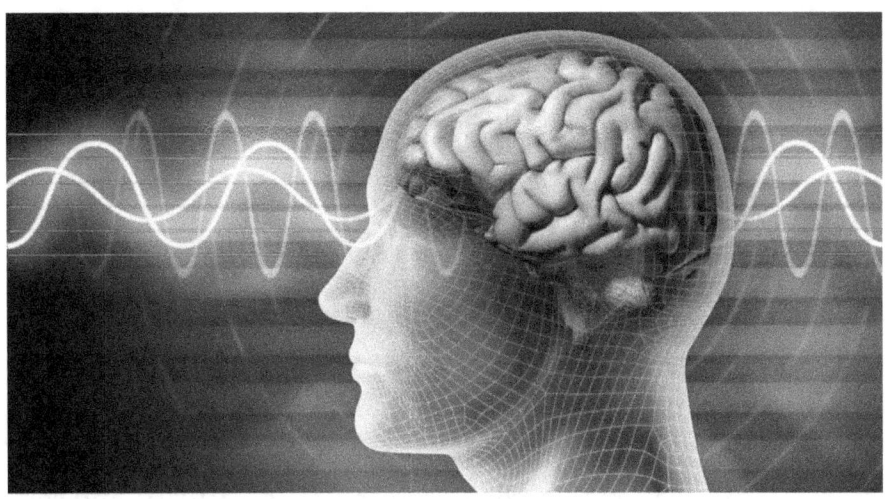

Chapter 5:

The Psychology Behind a Sale

Understanding the psychology behind a sale is crucial to mastering the art of selling. It is not simply about knowing the product or being able to recite a sales pitch; it is about comprehending the underlying human emotions, motivations, and behaviors that drive purchasing decisions.

Real-Life Anecdote: Steve Jobs and the Allure of Simplicity

Consider Steve Jobs, the co-founder of Apple. Jobs was not just selling computers; he was selling an experience, a lifestyle. He knew the psychological impact of design and simplicity and leveraged it to appeal to consumers' desire for beauty and ease of use. Apple products were positioned not just as gadgets but as gateways to creativity and innovation.

Understanding Consumer Behavior

Every sale begins with understanding what drives people to make a purchase. This understanding should form the basis of your daily routine. Each morning, take a moment to reflect on the previous day's interactions. What emotional cues did you observe? What motivated the customers to take action?

Training Program: Behavioral Insights

A comprehensive training program for understanding the psychology of sales might include:

1. **Behavioral Research**: Study the foundational theories of consumer behavior and psychology.

2. **Motivation Analysis**: Learn to recognize common motivational factors, such as status, security, and self-actualization.

3. **Emotional Intelligence Development**: Hone the ability to read and respond to emotional cues during sales interactions.

4. **Psychological Tactics Familiarization**: Familiarize yourself with psychological tactics such as scarcity, social proof, and reciprocity.

Daily Tasks and Training

1. **Case Study Analysis**: Review a sales case study daily, identifying the psychological factors at play.

2. **Role-Playing Scenarios**: Practice sales scenarios with a focus on understanding the customer's emotional and psychological state.

3. **Journaling Reflections**: Keep a journal to reflect on the psychological aspects observed during sales interactions.

4. **Learning New Tactics**: Dedicate time each week to learn a new psychological principle or sales tactic.

Actionable Strategies: Engaging the Mind

Incorporate these strategies to tap into the psychology of your customers:

- **Tell Stories**: Stories engage customers emotionally and can make the value of your product more relatable.

- **Create Urgency**: Limited-time offers can spur customers into making a decision more quickly.

- **Establish Authority**: Position yourself as an expert to increase trust and credibility.

- **Utilize Social Proof**: Use testimonials and reviews to show that others have had positive experiences.

Food for Thought: The Emotional Connection

Sales are as much about feeling as they are about logic. How can you create an emotional connection with your customers that goes beyond the product?

Summary: Harnessing Psychological Power

This chapter emphasized the following:

- **Emotional Intelligence**: Cultivating the ability to read and respond to customer emotions effectively.

- **Behavioral Understanding**: Gaining insights into what drives consumer behavior and purchasing decisions.

- **Psychological Techniques**: Learning and applying psychological tactics that can influence purchasing decisions.

- **Customer Connection**: Building a rapport that fosters trust and loyalty beyond the sale.

Homework:

1. Read a book on consumer psychology to deepen your understanding of buying behaviors.

2. Observe a sales interaction and identify the emotional and psychological drivers involved.

3. Implement one new psychological tactic in your sales approach and record its impact.

Further Reading:

- "Influence: The Psychology of Persuasion" by Robert B. Cialdini for a deeper understanding of the psychological principles that influence people's buying decisions.

- "Thinking, Fast and Slow" by Daniel Kahneman, which explores the dual systems that drive our thoughts and decisions in everyday life.

By the end of this chapter, you will have a foundational understanding of the complex interplay between emotion and logic in a sale. You'll be able to recognize psychological triggers and craft your sales approach to not only meet the needs but also to appeal to the inherent desires and behaviors of your customers, thereby increasing your effectiveness and sales outcomes.

Chapter 6:

Building Rapport and Trust Quickly

Trust is the foundation of any relationship, including the one between a salesperson and their customer. Without trust, no amount of persuasion or marketing strategy can be effective. Building rapport and trust quickly is a key skill that sets top salespeople apart from their peers.

Real-Life Anecdote: The Oprah Winfrey Effect

Oprah Winfrey is a prime example of someone who has mastered the art of building trust. Whether interviewing celebrities or endorsing products, she exudes sincerity and warmth, creating an immediate connection with her audience. Oprah's rapport with her guests and her audience is not by chance; it is the result of her genuine interest in people and her empathetic listening skills.

The Foundation of Trust

Trust is built on authenticity, consistency, and concern for the other person. Start each day with the intention of being fully present in your customer interactions. This means listening more than you talk and showing genuine interest in the person, not just the sale.

Training Program: Rapport Mastery

A training program focused on building rapport and trust might include:

1. **Active Listening Exercises**: Improve listening skills by focusing entirely on understanding the customer's perspective.

2. **Empathy Development**: Learn to see the world through your customer's eyes and respond with empathy.

3. **Authentic Communication Practices**: Practice communicating in a way that is true to yourself and resonates with others.

4. **Consistency Challenges**: Set challenges to ensure consistent follow-up and reliable customer service.

Daily Tasks and Training

1. **Mirroring Techniques**: Practice subtly mirroring your customer's body language and tone to create unconscious rapport.

2. **Personalization Exercises**: Start each day by planning how to personalize interactions with each customer.

3. **Feedback Sessions**: At the end of each day, seek feedback on your trust-building efforts from peers or mentors.

4. **Trust Building Actions**: Take at least one deliberate action each day to build or reinforce trust with a

customer.

Actionable Strategies: The Trust Formula

To build trust, integrate these strategies into every customer interaction:

- **Be Transparent**: Always communicate openly and honestly, even when the information is not favorable.
- **Show Consistency**: Be reliable in what you say and do; consistency breeds trust.
- **Provide Value**: Offer valuable information and insights, even if it doesn't lead to an immediate sale.
- **Follow Through**: Do what you say you will do, every single time.

Food for Thought: The Speed of Trust

Trust can be built quickly when intentions, words, and actions are aligned. How can you ensure alignment in all your interactions?

Summary: Quick Trust Building

This chapter outlined essential components for building rapport and trust quickly:

- **Active Listening**: Demonstrating that you hear and understand your customers' needs and concerns.
- **Authenticity**: Being genuine and truthful in every interaction.
- **Consistency**: Maintaining reliability in all customer engagements.
- **Value Offering**: Going beyond the sale to provide

something meaningful.

Homework:

1. Practice active listening in every conversation, focusing solely on the other person's words without planning your response.

2. Keep a journal of trust-building activities you undertake and the outcomes they produce.

3. Role-play difficult customer scenarios focusing on maintaining trust.

Further Reading:

- "The Speed of Trust" by Stephen M.R. Covey, which explores the power trust has on the effectiveness and success of relationships and organizations.

- "How to Win Friends and Influence People" by Dale Carnegie, a timeless guide on building relationships and influencing others.

By the end of this chapter, you'll have the tools and strategies needed to establish trust quickly and effectively. You'll be able to engage with customers in a way that demonstrates your commitment to their needs, making each sale not just a transaction, but the start of a long-lasting relationship.

Chapter 7:

Mastering the Art of Communication

Effective communication is the cornerstone of successful sales. Mastering this art means not only delivering your message but also ensuring it resonates and compels action. The most skilled salespeople are also master communicators—they know how to speak and listen in a way that builds relationships and drives sales.

Real-Life Anecdote: The Eloquence of Winston Churchill

Winston Churchill, the former British Prime Minister, is often celebrated for his oratory skills. His speeches during World War II weren't merely informative; they were inspiring and mobilizing. He knew the power of rhetoric, tone, and pause. He could communicate complex ideas simply and stir a nation to action. His ability to convey resolve and instill courage in his listeners was paramount to his leadership.

The Nuances of Sales Communication

Mastering communication in sales involves understanding the subtleties of language, non-verbal cues, and active listening. Every morning, as a daily ritual, rehearse your key messages, practicing clarity, brevity, and the art of persuasion.

Training Program: Communication Excellence

A training program aimed at honing communication skills might include:

1. **Rhetoric and Articulation**: Learn the techniques of great speakers and practice articulation exercises.

2. **Non-Verbal Communication**: Study body language and practice mirroring and congruence in gestures.

3. **Active Listening Skills**: Engage in exercises to develop the ability to listen actively and empathetically.

4. **Persuasive Speaking**: Familiarize yourself with the pillars of persuasion—ethos, pathos, and logos.

Daily Tasks and Training

1. **Speech Drills**: Begin each day with tongue twisters and vocal exercises to improve your diction and clarity.

2. **Non-Verbal Awareness**: Throughout the day, be consciously aware of your body language and what it communicates.

3. **Reflective Listening**: End each day by reflecting on your conversations—how well did you listen and respond to your customers?

4. **Message Refinement**: Regularly refine your sales messages based on customer feedback and your effectiveness.

Actionable Strategies: Communicative Impact

Adopt these strategies to enhance your communicative impact:

- **Tailor Your Message**: Customize your communication to resonate with your specific audience.

- **Simplify Complex Ideas**: Break down complex products or concepts into simple, relatable terms.

- **Use Analogies and Metaphors**: They can make ideas more vivid and memorable.

- **Practice Empathy**: Always consider the emotional state and perspective of your listener.

Food for Thought: The Echo of Words

How can you ensure that your words not only inform but also leave a lasting positive impression on your customers?

Summary: The Art of Sales Communication

In this chapter, we discussed critical elements of effective sales communication:

- **Clarity**: Being clear and concise in your message to avoid misunderstandings.

- **Non-Verbal Cues**: Using body language to reinforce your spoken words.

- **Active Listening**: Truly hearing your customer's needs and demonstrating understanding.

- **Persuasion**: Employing techniques to not only inform but also persuade.

Homework:

1. Record and listen to your sales pitch; evaluate your

    clarity, pace, and tone.

2. Observe a colleague's sales pitch and provide constructive feedback on their communication style.

3. Engage in a challenging conversation, focusing on maintaining clarity and composure.

Further Reading:

- "Made to Stick" by Chip and Dan Heath, which analyzes why some ideas survive and others die, offering insight into crafting compelling messages.

- "Talk Like TED" by Carmine Gallo, providing lessons from TED talks on effective communication.

After digesting this chapter, you will understand that selling is not just about what you say, but how you say it. With dedicated practice and reflection, you'll sharpen your ability to communicate persuasively, making every word count towards achieving your sales goals.

Chapter 8:

The Power of Storytelling in Sales

In the world of sales, facts and figures can inform, but stories are what truly persuade. Stories evoke emotion, build connections, and are remembered far longer than data. This chapter explores the transformative power of storytelling in sales and how to harness it to engage and convert any audience.

Real-Life Anecdote: Steve Jobs - The Storyteller

When you think of a riveting sales presentation, one might recall the iconic image of Steve Jobs unveiling a new Apple product. Jobs was not just selling a gadget; he was telling a story - one where his products were heroes that promised to revolutionize the listener's life. His presentations were masterclasses in storytelling, each element meticulously chosen to create an emotional arc that captivated the audience.

Why Stories Work

Neuroscience explains that our brains are wired to respond to stories. They activate parts of the brain associated with sight, sound, taste, and movement. They make us feel emotions and remember experiences. In sales, when you tell a story, you're not just speaking to a client's rational mind; you're engaging their emotions, and that's where decisions are truly made.

Training Program: Narrative Influence

A well-rounded storytelling training program for sales might include:

1. **The Elements of a Good Story**: Study the key components that make stories compelling.

2. **Building a Story Bank**: Learn how to collect and craft stories relevant to your products and audience.

3. **Storytelling Practice**: Regularly practice telling your stories and refining them based on listener feedback.

4. **Emotional Engagement**: Understand how to emotionally engage your audience through the narratives you tell.

Daily Tasks and Training

1. **Daily Storytelling**: Share a story with a colleague or friend every day to hone your skills.

2. **Customer Stories Collection**: After interactions with customers, jot down any anecdotes or outcomes that could be woven into a story.

3. **Observation Log**: Keep a log of successful storytelling you observe in your daily life, noting what made it effective.

4. **Story Analysis**: Break down stories from famous speakers or ads to understand their structure and

impact.

Actionable Strategies: Weaving Tales That Sell

Implement these strategies to integrate storytelling into your sales approach:

- **Start With the 'Why'**: Begin your story by explaining why the product matters, not just what it is or how it works.
- **Make It Relatable**: Craft stories that your audience can see themselves in.
- **Highlight the Transformation**: Focus on how your product changes situations or lives.
- **Use Vivid Imagery**: Paint a picture with your words to make the story come alive.

Food for Thought: Beyond the Narrative

As you develop your storytelling prowess, ask yourself, "What stories does my audience need to hear that they haven't heard before?"

Summary: Unleashing the Storyteller Within

This chapter has delved into:

- **The Science of Storytelling**: Why stories resonate with us on a deep level.
- **Components of Effective Stories**: What makes a story compelling and memorable.
- **Integrating Stories into Sales**: How to use storytelling to enhance your sales approach.
- **Practice and Refinement**: The importance of regular

storytelling practice and refinement.

Homework:

1. Develop three stories related to your product or service that highlight different benefits or outcomes.

2. Present a story to a peer and ask for feedback on the emotional and persuasive elements.

3. Identify a brand that uses storytelling effectively and analyze what makes it successful.

Further Reading:

- "Storynomics" by Robert McKee and Tom Gerace, which explains how to create stories that move and persuade in business.

- "The Storyteller's Secret" by Carmine Gallo, which shares storytelling strategies from the world's greatest leaders.

By understanding the power of storytelling in sales, you can move beyond mere transactions and forge meaningful connections with your audience. You'll learn not just to sell a product, but to tell a story that sells a vision, a dream, and ultimately, the promise of a better reality.

Chapter 9:

Overcoming Objections Gracefully

The path of a sales conversation is rarely obstacle-free. Objections are a natural part of the sales process, but how you handle them can make the difference between a lost sale and a loyal customer. In this chapter, we will explore the art of turning objections into opportunities, ensuring you handle them with poise and confidence.

Real-Life Anecdote: J.K. Rowling's Rejections

Before "Harry Potter" became a global phenomenon, J.K. Rowling faced numerous rejections. Publishers dismissed the manuscript as too long, too fantastical, or not commercially viable. Rowling didn't give up; she listened to the feedback, refined her pitch, and continued to present her work. Her perseverance and ability to overcome objections paid off spectacularly.

Understanding Objections

The first step in overcoming objections is to understand them. Objections often stem from a lack of information or a specific concern that has not been addressed. It's essential to view objections not as barriers but as the customer expressing interest in a deeper understanding of the product.

Training Program: The Graceful Art of Objection Handling

Developing a robust training program for overcoming objections involves:

1. **Objection Identification**: Learning to quickly identify the type of objection being presented.

2. **Active Listening Skills**: Training to listen actively and understand the underlying concerns.

3. **Objection Handling Techniques**: Mastering techniques to address and alleviate concerns.

4. **Role-Playing Scenarios**: Engaging in role-play to practice responses to common objections in a controlled environment.

Daily Tasks and Training

1. **Daily Objection Journal**: Write down objections encountered each day and reflect on how you addressed them.

2. **Role-Play Practice**: Daily role-play sessions with peers to simulate objection handling.

3. **Feedback Analysis**: Obtain feedback on your objection handling and use it to improve.

4. **Case Studies Review**: Analyze case studies of successful objection handling to learn from real-world examples.

Actionable Strategies: Turning 'No' Into 'Yes'

To overcome objections gracefully, implement the following strategies:

- **Empathize**: Acknowledge the customer's concerns to show you are listening and you care.
- **Clarify**: Ask questions to ensure you understand the objection fully.
- **Educate**: Provide information that addresses the objection directly.
- **Reframe**: Help the customer see the objection from a different, more positive perspective.
- **Confirm**: After addressing the objection, confirm with the customer that you have resolved their concern.

Food for Thought: Objections as Insight

Consider every objection as feedback. What can objections teach you about your product, your market, or your sales approach?

Summary: Embracing Objections

This chapter has covered:

- **Perspective on Objections**: Viewing objections as a natural and positive aspect of the sales conversation.
- **Types of Objections**: Understanding different objections and strategies for handling them.
- **Techniques for Overcoming Objections**: Practical methods to address and alleviate customer concerns.
- **Practice and Persistence**: The necessity of ongoing practice and persistence in handling objections.

Homework:

1. List the top five objections you face and develop a detailed response for each.

2. Conduct a 'worst-case scenario' role-play with a colleague, facing the most challenging objections.

3. Review a recent sales interaction where an objection was not overcome and identify what could have been done differently.

Further Reading:

- "Objections" by Jeb Blount, which provides insight into the emotional and psychological aspects of objection handling.

- "SPIN Selling" by Neil Rackham, where handling objections is part of the larger consultative selling approach.

By refining the skill of handling objections gracefully, you become not just a better salesperson but a trusted advisor. This chapter ensures that the next time you face an objection, you will see it as an opportunity to demonstrate the true value of your offering and strengthen your customer relationship.

Chapter 10:

The Strategic Sales Process

In the high-stakes game of sales, having a strategic process isn't just beneficial; it's imperative for success. Sales are not just about the gift of gab or the art of persuasion; it's about a meticulous, strategic approach that can be learned, refined, and perfected. This chapter delves into the strategic sales process, equipping you with a blueprint to sell anything, to anyone, at any time.

Real-Life Anecdote: The Precision of Jeff Bezos

Amazon's Jeff Bezos is a paragon of strategic processes. He didn't build one of the world's most successful companies by chance. Bezos's approach to sales and expansion was methodical. He started with books - a market vast enough to gain traction but focused enough to manage. He then used data, customer feedback, and market trends to strategically expand Amazon's offerings. Every move was calculated; every expansion was strategic.

Understanding the Strategic Sales Process

A strategic sales process breaks down the journey from prospecting to closing into specific, manageable stages, each with its own goals and methods. It's not a one-size-fits-all formula, but rather a flexible framework that adapts to different selling scenarios.

Training Program: Building a Strategic Sales Force

Creating a successful training program for a strategic sales process involves:

1. **Stages of Sales Mastery**: Understanding each stage of the sales process and its objectives.

2. **Customer Journey Mapping**: Learning to align sales strategies with the customer's buying journey.

3. **Data-Driven Decision Making**: Using data to inform and refine sales strategies.

4. **Continuous Improvement Workshops**: Regularly reviewing and improving sales tactics based on outcomes and feedback.

Daily Tasks and Training

1. **Prospecting Exercise**: Spend time each day identifying and researching potential leads.

2. **Sales Stage Review**: At the end of the day, review which stage each prospect is in and plan next steps.

3. **Customer Feedback Analysis**: Gather and analyze customer feedback to improve the sales approach.

4. **Peer Learning Sessions**: Share experiences with peers to learn from each other's strategies.

Actionable Strategies: The Five Pillars of Strategic Sales

1. **Prospecting**: Use strategic criteria to identify and target potential leads.

2. **Connecting**: Establish meaningful connections with prospects using tailored communication.

3. **Presenting**: Develop compelling presentations that address the specific needs and pain points of your audience.

4. **Closing**: Use a variety of closing techniques that fit the context and the customer.

5. **Following Up**: Implement a systematic follow-up process to ensure customer satisfaction and explore further opportunities.

Food for Thought: The Sales Process as a Learning Tool

Every interaction in the sales process is an opportunity to learn. How can each sale, successful or not, refine your sales strategy?

Summary: The Path to Sales Success

This chapter covered:

- **The Framework of a Strategic Sales Process**: The stages and elements of a structured approach to selling.

- **Alignment with the Buyer's Journey**: Tailoring the sales process to the customer's path to purchase.

- **Tactical Execution**: The implementation of specific strategies at each stage of the sales process.

- **The Importance of Adaptability**: Emphasizing the need to evolve the sales process in response to data and feedback.

Homework:

1. Develop a strategic sales plan for a product or service, outlining actions for each stage of the sales process.

2. Identify a recent sales interaction that did not result in a close and pinpoint which stage of the process could have been improved.

3. Create a customer journey map for your target demographic to better align your sales strategy.

Further Reading:

- "The Challenger Sale" by Matthew Dixon and Brent Adamson, which presents a new approach to selling tailored to the modern customer.

- "New Sales. Simplified." by Mike Weinberg, where a strategic approach to sales is distilled into actionable steps.

With a strategic sales process, you become a formidable force in the marketplace. This chapter arms you with the tools to not only navigate but also to master the sales terrain. Remember, in the landscape of sales, strategy is king, and with this knowledge, you're well on your way to wearing the crown.

Chapter 11:

Prospecting: Finding the Right Customers

The cornerstone of any successful sales strategy lies in the ability to prospect effectively. Prospecting, the act of identifying and reaching out to potential customers, is where the seed of every sale is planted. It is an art that combines research, intuition, and strategy to discover where your future customers will come from. This chapter will guide you through the intricacies of prospecting to ensure that you find not just any customer, but the right one.

Real-Life Anecdote: Ray Kroc and McDonald's Expansion

Ray Kroc, the mastermind behind the global expansion of McDonald's, was not the company's founder but its most successful prospector. He saw the potential in a single fast-food restaurant in San Bernardino, California, and turned it into an empire by prospecting nationwide for franchisees who shared his vision. Kroc's ability to identify the right partners for his business was instrumental in making McDonald's a household name.

The Essence of Prospecting

At its core, prospecting is about filtering through the masses to find the gold—the customers who are most likely to benefit from and purchase your product or service. It's about using a combination of data, social skills, and strategic thinking to connect with potential leads.

Training Program: Sharpening the Prospector's Eye

A training program aimed at enhancing prospecting skills would include:

1. **Market Research Fundamentals**: Understanding how to analyze the market to identify promising segments.
2. **Lead Generation Techniques**: Learning the most effective methods for generating a list of potential leads.
3. **Sales Intelligence Tools**: Training on how to use various sales tools to gather information on prospects.
4. **Networking and Referral Building**: Developing skills to network effectively and build a referral system.

Daily Tasks and Training

1. **Lead Research**: Dedicate time each day to researching new leads and gathering information about them.
2. **Cold Outreach**: Practice crafting and sending personalized outreach messages to potential prospects.
3. **Social Media Engagement**: Use social media platforms to connect with potential leads and engage with their

content.

4. **Prospecting Analysis**: End each day by reviewing the outcomes of your prospecting efforts and planning adjustments for the next day.

Actionable Strategies: Navigating the Prospecting Maze

- **Targeted Research**: Start with in-depth research to identify characteristics of your ideal customer.

- **Segmentation**: Break down your market into segments and tailor your prospecting approach to each.

- **Networking**: Attend industry events and engage online to expand your network.

- **Social Selling**: Use social media platforms not just to connect, but to understand and engage with potential prospects.

Food for Thought: The Human Element of Prospecting

Consider the personal touch in prospecting. How can understanding human behavior and building genuine relationships improve your prospecting success?

Summary: Prospecting with Purpose

We covered:

- **Prospecting Defined**: An overview of the purpose and importance of prospecting in the sales process.

- **Prospecting Strategies**: Different strategies for identifying and reaching out to potential customers.

- **Leveraging Technology**: How to use digital tools to aid in the prospecting process.

- **Best Practices**: The dos and don'ts of prospecting effectively.

Homework:

1. Identify and outline a profile for your ideal customer.
2. Create a strategic prospecting plan that includes daily, weekly, and monthly activities.
3. Role-play various prospecting scenarios with a colleague to refine your approach.

Further Reading:

- "Fanatical Prospecting" by Jeb Blount, which discusses the importance of proactive prospecting in the modern sales process.
- "Predictable Revenue" by Aaron Ross and Marylou Tyler, offering insight into creating a scalable prospecting system.

Prospecting is your first contact with potential success in sales. It's the foundation upon which deals are built and quotas are exceeded. Mastering the art of prospecting doesn't just mean more sales—it means better sales, stronger relationships, and a more robust business. Carry forward the lessons from this chapter, and watch as your client list—and your success—grows.

Chapter 12:

The First Impression: Opening the Conversation

In the realm of sales, the power of the first impression is undeniable. It can make or break a relationship and, by extension, a sale. The opening of a conversation is your unique opportunity to set the tone, establish credibility, and earn the right to hold your prospect's attention. This chapter unlocks the secrets to making your first impression not just good, but great.

Real-Life Anecdote: Oprah Winfrey's Unforgettable Introductions

Oprah Winfrey, a titan of media and a philanthropist, knows the value of a first impression. Her legendary talk show openings were as powerful as they were warm, inviting millions into her conversation. Oprah's ability to connect with her guests and audience from the very first moment is a testament to her mastery of the art of the opening.

The Importance of the Opening

The opening of your sales conversation is more than just a greeting; it's a strategic element of your overall sales process. It's where you begin to build trust, pique interest, and differentiate yourself from the competition.

Training Program: Mastering the Art of the Opening

A robust training program focused on crafting effective conversation openings would include:

1. **Introduction Techniques**: Learning various ways to introduce yourself and your value proposition effectively.

2. **Rapport Building**: Understanding how to quickly establish a connection with various types of clients.

3. **Communication Skills**: Enhancing verbal and nonverbal communication skills to make a powerful impact.

4. **Scenario Training**: Practicing opening conversations in different scenarios, from cold calls to high-stakes meetings.

Daily Tasks and Training

1. **Mirror Practice**: Rehearse your opening statements in front of a mirror, paying attention to body language and tone.

2. **Role-playing**: Engage in role-playing exercises to practice and refine your opening in a safe environment.

3. **Feedback Sessions**: Regularly record your opening pitches and critique them with a mentor or peer.

4. **Market Research**: Stay informed on current events and

industry trends to weave into your conversations for relevance and rapport.

Actionable Strategies: Crafting a Captivating Opening

- **Tailored Greetings**: Personalize your opening based on the prospect's background and interests.

- **Elevated Pitch**: Design an elevated pitch that succinctly conveys the core benefits of your product or service.

- **Curiosity Spark**: Start with an intriguing fact, statistic, or question that directly relates to the prospect's pain points.

- **Active Listening**: Open the door for the prospect to speak early on and listen intently to guide the conversation's direction.

Food for Thought: First Impressions and Lasting Relationships

How can a first impression be structured to lay the groundwork for a long-term relationship, not just a one-time sale?

Summary: The Art of the Opening

In this chapter, we explored:

- **The Role of the Opening**: Understanding the impact of the first impression in the sales conversation.

- **Opening Techniques**: Different methods for starting a sales conversation effectively.

- **The Power of Preparation**: The importance of preparing personalized openings for different prospects.

- **Practical Application**: Applying strategies for making

a great first impression in various sales scenarios.

Homework:

1. Craft three different opening statements for different types of prospects you encounter.

2. Analyze your last five sales conversations, focusing on how you opened each dialogue and the prospect's response.

3. Compile a list of opening lines from successful salespeople and identify what makes them effective.

Further Reading:

- "How to Win Friends and Influence People" by Dale Carnegie, for timeless advice on making impactful first impressions.

- "Influence: The Psychology of Persuasion" by Robert Cialdini, which can help you understand how to become more persuasive from the first moment of contact.

Opening a conversation effectively is a critical skill in sales that goes far beyond a simple hello. It's an opportunity to establish yourself as a professional, to stand out, and to start the sales process off on the right foot. Use this chapter as your guide to mastering your openings, and each new conversation will bring a world of potential.

Chapter 13:

Qualifying Leads: Is This a Potential Sale?

Qualifying leads effectively is the backbone of a productive sales strategy. It's about asking the right questions to determine whether there's a genuine opportunity for a sale. Without this critical step, a salesperson risks wasting valuable time and resources on leads that will never convert. This chapter delves into the crucial skill of lead qualification, ensuring your sales efforts are targeted and effective.

Real-Life Anecdote: Steve Jobs and the Precise Art of Lead Qualification

Steve Jobs, the late co-founder of Apple, was a master at identifying and focusing on leads that mattered. He did not just market to anyone; he targeted those who yearned for innovation, ease of use, and design—traits that Apple products exemplified. His approach was to create and cater to a specific audience, one that was qualified and more likely to convert into loyal customers.

Understanding Lead Qualification

Lead qualification is a systematic process of assessing whether a prospect can and will make a purchase. It's about understanding their needs, budget, authority, timing, and the extent to which your product or service solves a problem for them.

Training Program: Honing Lead Qualification Skills

A comprehensive training program for lead qualification would include modules on:

1. **Identifying Buyer Personas**: Understanding the characteristics of an ideal buyer for your product or service.

2. **Questioning Techniques**: Learning to ask probing questions that uncover the lead's true intent and capability.

3. **Listening Skills**: Developing the ability to listen actively to what the lead is implicitly and explicitly saying.

4. **Analyzing Responses**: Training on interpreting the information provided by the lead to make an informed qualification decision.

Daily Tasks and Training

1. **Prospect Research**: Spend time each day researching prospects to understand their potential fit.

2. **Qualification Drills**: Practice with mock calls or with a colleague to refine your qualification questioning.

3. **Reviewing Interactions**: Analyze past sales calls to identify cues that indicated a lead's qualification

status.

4. **Staying Informed**: Keep up with industry and market trends that may affect the qualification process.

Actionable Strategies: Effective Lead Qualification

- **BANT Framework**: Utilize the BANT (Budget, Authority, Need, Timing) framework to guide your qualification questions.

- **Solution-Oriented Dialogue**: Engage in conversations that focus on how your product can solve the lead's problem.

- **Record Keeping**: Maintain detailed records of interactions with leads to assess qualification over time.

- **Disqualification Criteria**: Understand and recognize when to disqualify a lead to avoid wasting time.

Food for Thought: The Ethical Dimension of Qualification

How do you balance aggressive sales tactics with ethical considerations during lead qualification?

Summary: The Science of Qualification

In this chapter, we covered:

- **The Importance of Qualification**: Explaining why qualifying leads is a critical step in the sales process.

- **Strategies for Qualification**: Discussing various techniques for effectively qualifying leads.

- **Practical Application**: How to apply qualification techniques in real-world scenarios.

- **Assessment and Adaptation**: Continuously assessing

and refining your lead qualification approach.

Homework:

1. Create a list of qualification questions tailored to your product and intended customer base.

2. Role-play a qualification scenario with a colleague, then provide feedback to each other.

3. Develop a checklist for identifying a qualified lead based on industry benchmarks and past successful sales.

Further Reading:

- "SPIN Selling" by Neil Rackham, for insights on asking the right questions in the sales process.

- "The Challenger Sale" by Matthew Dixon and Brent Adamson, which offers a new perspective on qualifying leads and driving sales.

Effective lead qualification is not just about discerning who can buy, but who should buy. By focusing on qualifying leads, you ensure that your sales energy is spent on prospects who are most likely to become customers, maximizing efficiency and success. With the strategies outlined in this chapter, you are well-equipped to transform your qualification process into a precise, value-driven effort.

Chapter 14:

Presenting Like a Pro

In the journey of a sale, the presentation is your moment on stage—it's where the curtain rises on your product or service and the spotlight shines on your offering. But this isn't just about showcasing a product; it's a performance that, if done correctly, leads to a standing ovation and an encore in the form of a closed deal.

The Pro Presenter: Oprah Winfrey

Oprah Winfrey, a name synonymous with charismatic communication and inspirational dialogue, didn't reach her status by mere chance. Her follow-up strategies were as much a part of her path to success as her talent. After every significant interview or meeting, Oprah made it a point to send a thank you note, a gesture that not only showed gratitude but kept the communication lines open for future opportunities. It was this kind of meticulous attention to the follow-up that transformed one-time guests into lifelong friends and collaborators.

Deepening Strategy Explanations

Timely Follow-Up: Oprah knew the importance of timeliness. A prompt follow-up indicates to the client that they are a priority and that you are serious about your business. This strategy isn't about being first; it's about being considered.

Training Recommendations:

- **Follow-Up Drills**: Simulate a sales process with a peer and practice sending timely follow-up messages.
- **Response Time Analysis**: Record how long it takes you to follow up with leads and work on reducing this time while maintaining message quality.

Personalization: Just as Oprah would tailor her interviews to each guest, sales follow-ups should be customized. Use the details from initial meetings to show that you are paying attention and value the client's unique needs.

Training Recommendations:

- **Client History Review**: Study past interactions before following up. Remind yourself of personal tidbits shared by the client.
- **Customized Communication Practice**: Craft follow-up messages based on specific details from previous conversations.

Adding Value: Oprah often followed up with additional information or thoughtful gifts that related to the conversation she had with her guests. Every follow-up should provide additional value—be it a relevant article, a helpful tip, or an industry insight.

Training Recommendations:

- **Value Identification Exercise**: Identify what additional value you can offer your client beyond your initial meeting.
- **Resourcefulness Development**: Keep up with industry news and trends to have a repository of value-adds at your disposal.

Real-Life Examples and Techniques Explored

Steve Jobs' Follow-Up Persistence: After initial talks with music industry executives for what would become iTunes, Jobs didn't just wait for responses—he followed up. He knew that his persistence would keep the conversation going and demonstrate his commitment.

Training Recommendations:

- **Persistence Role-Playing**: Practice follow-up scenarios where persistence is key, and develop techniques to keep the client engaged.
- **Creative Persistence Planning**: Map out a follow-up timeline that includes multiple touchpoints without being overwhelming.

Homework Assignments

1. **Follow-Up Campaign Development**: Create a campaign for your product or service with multiple follow-up touchpoints.
2. **Client Simulation**: Partner with a colleague to act as a

client. Execute your follow-up campaign and refine it based on feedback.

3. **Case Studies Analysis**: Review successful sales campaigns and identify the follow-up strategies that made them successful.

Food for Thought: Consider how you perceive follow-up communications when you're the customer. What frequency and type of follow-up do you find valuable versus intrusive?

Summary: Key Takeaways

1. Follow up promptly and regularly.
2. Personalize your follow-up communications to build rapport.
3. Each follow-up should provide additional value.
4. Emulate successful follow-up strategies from renowned communicators like Oprah Winfrey and Steve Jobs.

In this chapter, "The Pro Presenter: Oprah Winfrey" serves as the linchpin, exemplifying that the art of following up is about fostering relationships and ensuring continuity. The provided strategies, training recommendations, and homework assignments are designed to help readers implement a follow-up approach that aligns with their sales style while remaining effective and client-centric. The real-life examples inspire readers to see the follow-up not as a post-sale formality but as an integral step in the sales process, encouraging them to approach it with the same creativity and commitment as their sales presentations.

Understanding the Art of Presentation

Presentation is an art form, and those who have mastered it understand that it's about weaving a narrative that resonates with the audience. The key lies not just in what you're selling, but how you deliver the message.

Deepening Strategy Explanations

Engage with Stories: Just as a painter uses every stroke to create an emotional response, a presenter uses stories to engage and connect. The most successful presenters know that stories are the pathway to the audience's heart and mind.

Training Recommendations:

- **Daily Storytelling Practice**: Commit to telling a new story each day, whether to a friend, a colleague, or even in front of a mirror.
- **Story Bank Creation**: Compile a diverse collection of stories, anecdotes, and analogies that you can draw upon relevant to different sales scenarios.

Active Listening: The art of presentation is as much about listening as it is about speaking. Great presenters like Larry King believed that an interview's success largely depended on the ability to listen actively and respond to the interviewee.

Training Recommendations:

- **Listening Exercises**: Spend a portion of your day actively listening to others without trying to formulate a response.
- **Feedback Implementation**: After a presentation, ask for feedback on how well you responded to the

audience's verbal and nonverbal cues.

Real-Life Examples and Techniques Explored

Steve Jobs' Presentation Mastery: Steve Jobs wasn't just selling technology; he was selling a dream, an experience. He demonstrated that understanding the product's design and impact is crucial to a successful presentation.

Training Recommendations:

- **Design Thinking Workshops**: Take part in or conduct workshops that focus on product design and user experience to enhance your understanding.
- **Emulate Presentation Styles**: Study videos of Jobs' presentations and practice his style—how he used pauses, emphasized certain words, and interacted with the product.

Homework Assignments

1. **Presentation Recording and Review**: Record your sales presentations and critically review them, focusing on body language, storytelling, and how well you adapted your message to the audience's reactions.
2. **Peer Presentation Sessions**: Organize sessions with peers where each gets a turn to present and receive constructive feedback.
3. **Learning from the Masters**: Select a presenter you admire, watch several of their presentations, and write an analysis of their techniques.

Food for Thought: If a presentation were a canvas, what colors would your words be? How does your delivery add or detract from the picture you're trying to paint for your audience?

Summary: Key Takeaways

1. Utilize storytelling to make your presentations engaging and memorable.
2. Active listening is crucial; tailor your presentation in real-time based on audience feedback.
3. Learn from the presentation styles of masters like Steve Jobs and incorporate their techniques into your style.
4. Continuous practice and feedback are key to improving your presentation skills.

In "Understanding the Art of Presentation," the focus is on the power of storytelling, the necessity of active listening, and the importance of continuous learning and adaptation. This section not only guides readers through developing their presentation skills but also encourages them to become students of their craft by learning from the greats. The real-life anecdotes and examples are designed to inspire and provide a framework that readers can directly apply to their daily tasks and training programs. This chapter goes beyond the theoretical to ensure readers have actionable strategies that lead to mastery in the art of presentation.

Training Program: Developing Presentation Skills

Deepened Strategy Explanations

In-depth presentation skills are foundational to selling effectively. This training program is designed to refine these skills through daily practices, actionable strategies, and learning from the experts.

Developing a Compelling Narrative: The best sales presentations tell a story, one where the customer is the hero, and your product or service is the key to their success.

- **Daily Task**: Each day, take a feature of your product and create a short story around how it solves a specific problem.
- **Training Recommendation**: Enroll in a storytelling workshop and regularly practice your storytelling in different scenarios to adapt your skills.

Dynamic Delivery: How you deliver your presentation can be just as important as what you deliver. Your voice, pacing, and body language communicate confidence and conviction.

- **Daily Task**: Record a video of yourself presenting and watch it back, noting areas for improvement.
- **Training Recommendation**: Take voice modulation and public speaking courses, and practice these techniques in your daily conversations, not just formal presentations.

Real-Life Examples and Technique Exploration

Using Humor like Ellen DeGeneres: Ellen uses humor to engage her audience, making complex or dry topics more relatable and memorable.

- **Training Recommendation**: Study a few segments from "The Ellen Show". Notice how she introduces humor into her conversations. Try incorporating light-hearted comments or anecdotes into your presentations.

Michelle Obama's Emotional Connection: The former First

Lady is known for her ability to connect emotionally with her audience, creating a rapport that enhances her message.

- **Training Recommendation**: Watch Michelle Obama's speeches, focusing on how she uses personal stories to create emotional connections. Try sharing personal experiences in your presentations to create a bond with your audience.

Homework Assignments

1. **Narrative Development**: Write out the "hero's journey" for three different customer profiles with your product as the "magical tool" they need.
2. **Public Speaking Engagement**: Sign up for a local Toastmasters meeting or similar public speaking group to practice your delivery.
3. **Humor Implementation**: Incorporate humor into at least one presentation each week, no matter how small.

Food for Thought:

How does your presentation make your audience feel? Do they see themselves in the story you're telling? Are they moved to action by the narrative you've woven?

Summary: Key Takeaways

1. Craft compelling narratives that position your customers as the hero.
2. Focus on dynamic delivery to keep your audience engaged.
3. Learn from accomplished presenters and integrate their techniques into your style.

4. Commit to a rigorous routine of practice, feedback, and adaptation.

In this section, "Training Program: Developing Presentation Skills," the strategies and daily tasks are crafted to help readers evolve their presentation skills into an art form. By offering a structured training regimen supported by real-life examples of successful presenters, readers are encouraged to analyze and emulate the techniques that resonate with them. From developing a compelling narrative to delivering it with confidence and finesse, the program provides a holistic approach to mastering the presentation skills essential in sales. This chapter ensures that readers are not only given strategies but are also shown how to implement these strategies in a practical, daily format that promotes growth and skill enhancement.

Actionable Strategies: Winning Presentation Techniques

Deepened Strategy Explanations

Presentations are pivotal moments in the sales process; hence, winning presentation techniques go beyond the content. It involves mastering the art of engagement, storytelling, and persuasive rhetoric.

1. The Power of Pausing:

Like a skilled composer, a presenter must know when to pause, to emphasize points, and to let the audience absorb information.

- **Daily Task**: Practice speaking on a topic, intentionally incorporating pauses after making a point.

- **Training Recommendation**: Observe speeches by Barack Obama, who uses strategic pauses to great effect.

2. Invoking Curiosity:

Use rhetorical questions or provocative statements to pique interest.

- **Daily Task**: Start your team meetings with a thought-provoking question related to the day's agenda.
- **Training Recommendation**: Read "Made to Stick" by Chip and Dan Heath to understand how to make ideas resonate.

Real-Life Examples and Technique Exploration

Elon Musk's Visionary Presentations: Musk's presentations on SpaceX and Tesla are not just about the features of a rocket or a car; they paint the picture of a future that the audience can be a part of.

- **Real-Life Anecdote**: Musk once began a presentation by stating the probability of failure. This honesty not only captured attention but also set the stage for highlighting the audacious goals of SpaceX.
- **Training Recommendation**: Reflect on your product's vision and how it can shape the future. Craft your presentation to share this vision as a story where the audience plays a critical role.

Steve Jobs' Simplified Complexity: Apple's product launches under Jobs were masterclasses in simplifying complex technology into digestible chunks that highlighted benefits over features.

- **Real-Life Anecdote**: When introducing the first iPhone, Jobs didn't start with tech specs; he began by framing it as three devices in one – a touch iPod, a revolutionary mobile phone, and a breakthrough

Internet communicator.

- **Training Recommendation**: For each feature of your product, find a benefit that your customer can relate to. Present the feature with the benefit as the headline.

Homework Assignments

1. **Visualization Exercise**: For every feature of your product, visualize a scenario where it solves a problem or adds value to your customer. Write it down as a mini-story.

2. **Tech-to-Benefit Translation**: Take a complex feature of your product and explain it in three sentences to a friend outside of your industry, focusing solely on benefits.

Food for Thought:

Are you selling a product, or are you offering a key to a new lifestyle, a door to opportunities, or peace of mind? How does your presentation reflect this?

Summary: Key Takeaways

1. Master the power of pausing to let your key points sink in.

2. Invoke curiosity to keep your audience engaged and wanting more.

3. Emulate visionaries like Musk and Jobs by framing your product in the context of a larger narrative or by simplifying complexity.

4. Regularly put into practice the techniques of visual storytelling and benefit translation to refine your presentation skills.

In the section "Actionable Strategies: Winning Presentation Techniques," we dive deeper into the nuanced skills that can make or break a sales presentation. The goal is to enable readers to adopt a more sophisticated approach to presenting, leveraging the tactics of industry giants who have famously captivated audiences. By studying the methods of people like Elon Musk and Steve Jobs, sales professionals can learn how to elevate their presentations from informative to inspirational.

The strategies provided are meant to be actionable, with clear daily tasks and training recommendations that allow for incremental improvement and the development of a compelling presenting style. The techniques highlighted here are intended to encourage readers to think beyond the basics of presentation, focusing on the delivery, engagement, and the overarching story that will resonate with their audience. This chapter emphasizes that the best sales presentations are not just about conveying information, but about creating an experience that aligns with the aspirations and needs of the audience.

Food for Thought: Selling Without 'Selling'

How can you present your product in such a way that the sale becomes a natural conclusion rather than a hard pitch?

Summary: The Makings of a Masterful Presentation

In summing up this chapter, we have covered:

- **The Role of Presentations in Sales**: Establishing why presentations are a critical element in the sales process.

- **Elements of a Successful Presentation**: Outlining the key components that make a presentation effective.

- **Techniques for Engagement**: Discussing methods to

keep your audience engaged and interested.

- **Continuous Improvement**: The importance of refining your presentation skills over time.

Homework:

1. Develop a presentation script for your product, focusing on a strong opening and closing.

2. Incorporate at least one personal or customer story that highlights the value of your offering.

3. Gather a set of tools and resources that will help you present more effectively, such as software, apps, or books on presentation skills.

Further Reading:

- "Talk Like TED" by Carmine Gallo, which dissects the success behind impactful TED Talks.

- "Slide:ology" by Nancy Duarte, for insights into creating visually compelling presentation slides.

As a sales professional, your ability to present effectively can make or break a deal. By embracing the strategies and insights presented in this chapter, you're equipping yourself with the tools needed to captivate and persuade any audience. Presenting like a pro isn't just about selling—it's about delivering an experience that aligns so closely with the audience's needs and desires that they can't help but want to be part of the story you're telling.

Chapter 15:

*Handling Sales Meetings
with Confidence*

Deepened Strategy Explanations

Sales meetings can be the linchpin to closing deals. Confidence in these meetings stems from thorough preparation, understanding the client, and being adept at real-time problem-solving.

1. The Socratic Method: This ancient technique involves asking questions to help the other person think through issues, making it a powerful tool in sales to understand client needs and concerns.

- **Daily Task**: Engage a colleague in a discussion about a common topic and only ask questions to guide the conversation.

- **Training Recommendation**: Study Plato's "Dialogues" to see the Socratic method in action.

2. Active Listening: Truly understanding what the client is saying, including the subtext, can reveal their true concerns and needs.

- **Daily Task**: In every conversation, summarize the other person's points to ensure understanding.
- **Training Recommendation**: Attend a workshop on active listening or engage with online courses that focus on communication skills.

Real-Life Examples and Technique Exploration

Richard Branson's Empathy in Communication: Branson, known for his charismatic leadership, exemplifies confidence in sales meetings by showing genuine interest and empathy.

- **Real-Life Anecdote**: Branson often shares personal stories, making his interactions memorable. Once, he turned a potentially negative meeting about a failed service into a collaborative session on improvements by actively engaging with customers' stories.
- **Training Recommendation**: In every meeting, find a way to relate to the client's experience personally. Practice this by sharing relevant personal stories that build empathy and trust.

Sheryl Sandberg's Focus on Solutions: The COO of Facebook, Sheryl Sandberg, is known for her solution-oriented approach, turning challenges into opportunities during sales discussions.

- **Real-Life Anecdote**: Sandberg addressed potential privacy concerns in a meeting with advertisers by proactively outlining Facebook's commitment and solutions, turning skepticism into confidence in the platform.

- **Training Recommendation**: Before every sales meeting, prepare a list of potential concerns the client may have and your solutions.

Homework Assignments

1. **Socratic Exercise**: Each day, pick a new product feature and think of five questions that lead a customer to understand its value.

2. **Empathy Building**: Write down a recent client interaction and identify areas where showing empathy could have changed the outcome.

Food for Thought: How can you ensure your sales meetings are not just transactions but the beginning of a relationship built on understanding and trust?

Summary: Key Takeaways

1. Use the Socratic method to guide clients to their own conclusions about your product's value.

2. Practice active listening to fully understand client needs and read between the lines.

3. Emulate leaders like Branson and Sandberg by employing empathy and focusing on solutions.

4. Continuously refine your approach with daily tasks and targeted training to handle sales meetings with unshakable confidence.

In the section "Handling Sales Meetings with Confidence," we delve into the subtleties of client interaction, emphasizing preparation and in-the-moment agility. The strategies are designed to foster a sense of confidence that is contagious, helping clients feel secure in their decisions.

By incorporating the methods of figures like Richard Branson and Sheryl Sandberg, sales professionals can learn to navigate meetings with a blend of empathy and strategic foresight. The suggested daily tasks and training programs are tailored to build the necessary skills gradually, encouraging a deeper connection with clients that goes beyond mere selling.

The emphasis on the Socratic method and active listening serves as the foundation for a consultative selling approach. The real-life anecdotes illustrate how these strategies play out in practice, offering models for sales professionals to emulate. This section aims to transform sales meetings from daunting tasks into opportunities for forging meaningful business relationships and securing sales through genuine connection and confidence.

Steve Jobs: The Epitome of Confidence

Steve Jobs stands as a paragon of confidence in sales meetings. His charisma and certainty not only sold products but sold dreams. He transformed the pitch into a vision-sharing experience, one where his belief was so palpable, it became contagious. His advice? "Have the courage to follow your heart and intuition."

Understanding the Dynamics of Sales Meetings

Deepened Strategy Explanations

Sales meetings are dynamic engagements where the energy, attitude, and strategy of the salesperson can pivot the outcome. It's not just about presenting a pitch; it's about reading the room, adapting the message, managing objections, and steering the conversation towards a mutual goal.

1. **Reading the Room**: This involves picking up on non-

verbal cues, understanding group dynamics, and adjusting your approach accordingly.

- **Daily Task**: Practice by observing people's reactions in various settings (cafes, meetings) and jot down your observations.

- **Training Recommendation**: Participate in improvisation classes to sharpen your ability to adapt to unscripted scenarios.

2. Adjusting the Message: Tailoring the conversation in real-time based on the audience's reactions is crucial for keeping them engaged.

- **Daily Task**: Create a flexible pitch for your product with multiple entry points depending on audience interest.

- **Training Recommendation**: Study communication techniques that focus on persuasive messaging and narrative flexibility.

Real-Life Examples and Technique Exploration

Steve Jobs' Charismatic Presentations: Jobs was a master at reading his audience, knowing when to unveil a product's features based on the crowd's energy.

- **Real-Life Anecdote**: During the first iPhone launch, Jobs intently watched the audience and paced his revelations to build excitement and climax.

- **Training Recommendation**: Analyze videos of Steve Jobs' product launches. Observe his timing, the buildup of his points, and his audience interaction.

Indra Nooyi's Adaptable Communication: As the former CEO of PepsiCo, Nooyi had the knack for adjusting her message for different stakeholders, from investors to consumers.

- **Real-Life Anecdote**: Nooyi once shifted a conversation from financials to health and wellness mid-meeting to align with her audience's shift in focus.

- **Training Recommendation**: Role-play various stakeholder meetings with colleagues, practicing how to shift your message based on different interests.

Homework Assignments

1. **Observation Log**: Keep a daily log of non-verbal cues observed in your interactions and reflect on how these could impact a sales meeting.

2. **Pitch Adaptation Exercise**: Draft three versions of your sales pitch tailored to different audience types.

Food for Thought: In what ways can you remain authentic while also flexibly adapting your sales approach to match the client's company culture and values?

Summary: Key Takeaways

1. Sharpen your ability to 'read the room' to create a receptive atmosphere.

2. Learn to adjust your messaging on-the-fly to keep engagement high.

3. Take inspiration from successful leaders like Jobs and Nooyi in handling the dynamics of meetings.

4. Embed flexibility and adaptability into your daily practice to navigate sales meetings effectively.

In "Understanding the Dynamics of Sales Meetings," the

focal point is the nuanced understanding of interactional undercurrents that define successful sales encounters. The strategies outlined encourage a dual approach of keen observation and responsive communication, ensuring that sales meetings are not just presentations but dialogues tailored to the clients' real-time feedback and energy.

We delve deeper into the psychology of group dynamics, giving sales professionals a playbook for navigating the complexities of varying audience types. The section offers actionable guidance on reading non-verbal cues, a skill exemplified by the likes of Steve Jobs, whose product presentations became legendary for their audience engagement.

With daily tasks designed to improve observational skills and training recommendations aimed at enhancing adaptability, this section is intended as a blueprint for turning every sales meeting into an opportunity to connect and resonate with clients on a deeper level. The real-life anecdotes provide tangible examples of these strategies in action, inspiring sales professionals to integrate these practices into their routines, ensuring they approach each sales meeting with a nuanced understanding and the confidence to adjust their strategy dynamically.

Training Program for Sales Meeting Mastery

Deepened Strategy Explanations

To master sales meetings, one must transcend basic presentation skills and adopt a holistic approach that includes strategic preparation, advanced communication skills, and post-meeting analysis.

Strategic Preparation: This is the groundwork that involves researching the client, their business, and the market context.

- **Daily Task**: Dedicate time each day to study industry trends and news that could affect your clients.
- **Training Recommendation**: Attend workshops on strategic business analysis to enhance your ability to understand diverse business environments.

Advanced Communication Skills: These are necessary to articulate your value proposition clearly and compellingly.

- **Daily Task**: Practice your pitch daily, focusing on clarity, brevity, and adaptability.
- **Training Recommendation**: Enroll in advanced sales communication courses that focus on persuasive language and high-impact delivery.

Post-meeting Analysis: After each meeting, review your performance and the client's feedback to refine your approach.

- **Daily Task**: Record your sales meetings (with permission) and critique your delivery and tactics afterward.
- **Training Recommendation**: Participate in peer review sessions where you can get constructive feedback on your performance.

Real-Life Examples and Technique Exploration

Warren Buffett's Annual Meetings: Known for his insightful and candid shareholder meetings, Buffett's preparation and understanding of his audience set him apart.

- **Real-Life Anecdote**: Buffett prepares for his meetings by anticipating the questions he might be asked and weaving relevant stories and humor into his answers.

- **Training Recommendation**: Analyze recordings of Buffett's shareholder meetings to understand how he engages with his audience and handles complex questions with ease.

Sheryl Sandberg's Engaging Dialogues: As a leader, Sandberg excels in creating a dialogue rather than a monologue in her meetings.

- **Real-Life Anecdote**: Sandberg often starts meetings with a personal anecdote that relates to the business at hand, making her approach relatable and engaging.

- **Training Recommendation**: Practice engaging storytelling that connects personal experiences to business scenarios.

Homework Assignments

1. **Client Case Studies**: Regularly write up case studies on your clients and potential leads to deepen your understanding of their needs.

2. **Pitch Practice Sessions**: Hold weekly pitch sessions with a colleague or mentor to refine your delivery and receive feedback.

Food for Thought: How can your sales meetings become a platform for storytelling that engages, informs, and compels action?

Summary: Key Takeaways

1. Adopt a strategy of continuous learning about your clients and their industries.

2. Develop communication skills that allow you to articulate your message powerfully and persuasively.

3. Implement a systematic approach to post-meeting analysis to continually refine your techniques.

4. Draw inspiration from successful communicators like Buffett and Sandberg to enhance engagement in meetings.

In the "Training Program for Sales Meeting Mastery" section, we take a comprehensive approach to mastering the intricacies of sales meetings. The strategies provided are designed to ensure that the salesperson is not just prepared but deeply connected with the client's world, able to communicate effectively and pivot as needed throughout the meeting.

The added depth comes from integrating real-life success stories into the fabric of training, such as Warren Buffett's methodical yet personable approach to shareholder meetings and Sheryl Sandberg's capacity to turn meetings into engaging narratives. The daily tasks and training recommendations are curated to build a habit of excellence, focusing on continuous improvement and strategic engagement.

The homework assignments are practical exercises that reinforce the learnings, ensuring that the salesperson remains at the top of their game. This section's strategies and anecdotes serve as a blueprint for sales professionals aiming to turn their meetings into a competitive advantage, fostering confidence and competence that can significantly impact their success rates.

Daily Tasks for Building Confidence

Deepened Strategy Explanations

Building confidence for sales meetings is not an overnight feat; it's a muscle that requires daily conditioning. Here's a deeper look into strategies to build this confidence:

Visualization: Visualization is not just a motivational tool but a cognitive rehearsal practice. Visualizing successful meetings stimulates the same neural networks as physically experiencing the meeting.

- **Daily Task**: Spend 10 minutes each morning visualizing a successful sales meeting, from greeting the client to answering tough questions with aplomb.

- **Detailed Explanation**: Imagine the room, the faces of your clients, your presentation material, and most importantly, your emotions. Feel the confidence and satisfaction of a well-executed meeting.

Self-Talk: What we say to ourselves can either be a powerful boost or a detrimental critic. Positive self-talk can increase your confidence and decrease stress.

- **Daily Task**: Replace every negative thought with two positive affirmations about your abilities and past successes.

- **Detailed Explanation**: Keep a journal of positive affirmations and success stories that you can refer to when you need a confidence boost.

Knowledge Building: Confidence comes from knowing your product or service inside out. This involves staying updated with all the latest information, trends, and potential objections.

- **Daily Task**: Allocate time to read about industry updates, new product features, or service protocols.

- **Detailed Explanation**: Use this knowledge to anticipate potential questions and concerns from your clients, allowing you to prepare responses in advance.

Role-Playing: Practice makes perfect, and role-playing is a technique that helps you prepare for various scenarios in a sales meeting.

- **Daily Task**: Engage in role-playing exercises with a peer or mentor, where you practice different parts of your sales meeting, from the opening to handling objections.

- **Detailed Explanation**: Record these sessions to review your language, body language, and the fluidity of your responses.

Real-Life Examples and Technique Exploration

Steve Jobs' Rehearsals: The late Apple CEO was known for his charismatic presentations. Jobs would spend hours rehearsing every aspect of his presentation to appear effortless.

- **Real-Life Anecdote**: It's reported that Jobs would rehearse for hundreds of hours before a product launch, fine-tuning every gesture and word.

- **Training Recommendation**: Simulate high-pressure presentation environments to practice staying calm and confident.

Food for Thought: Consider how top athletes spend their off-season training for the game. How can you adopt a similar 'training regimen' to master sales meetings?

Summary: Key Takeaways

1. Visualization can be as powerful as actual experience when it comes to mental preparation.

2. Positive self-talk is a critical tool for maintaining a confident mindset.

3. In-depth product knowledge and industry awareness serve as the foundation for confidence.

4. Role-playing prepares you for real-world scenarios, making you more adaptable and quick-thinking.

5. Draw inspiration from iconic figures like Steve Jobs, who exemplified the power of preparation and practice.

In the "Daily Tasks for Building Confidence" section, the approach is to integrate holistic methods that combine mental and practical exercises to build a salesperson's confidence progressively. These tasks are not just actions but a discipline aimed at improving the mental, emotional, and intellectual facets of a salesperson's profile.

Through the lens of Steve Jobs' meticulous preparation rituals, we understand the importance of rehearsal and fine-tuning every detail. This section advocates for a regimen that cultivates a sense of readiness and poise, which is vital in high-stakes sales environments.

Each task and recommendation is designed to transform the salesperson's daily routine into a comprehensive training program, with each component playing a crucial role in shaping a well-rounded, confident sales expert. The food for thought encourages salespeople to draw parallels between themselves and top-performing professionals in any field, emphasizing the universality of preparation and self-belief in achieving excellence.

Actionable Strategies for Effective Sales Meetings

Deepened Strategy Explanations

Effective sales meetings are the culmination of excellent preparation, strategic thinking, and interpersonal skills. Here's an enhanced explanation of the strategies that lead to successful sales meetings:

Tailored Value Communication: Your product or service must be presented in a way that resonates personally with the client's needs.

- **Daily Task**: Research one client a day, diving into their business, their challenges, and potential aspirations.
- **Detailed Explanation**: Use this information to tailor your sales pitch, focusing on how your product can solve specific problems or help them achieve their goals.

Building Credibility: Trust is the currency of sales, and credibility is how you earn it. Credibility comes from demonstrating expertise, understanding the client's industry, and showing reliability.

- **Daily Task**: Develop and share content related to your field, such as blog posts, case studies, or industry analyses, which can provide value to your clients.
- **Detailed Explanation**: This practice positions you as a thought leader and a trusted advisor rather than just a salesperson.

Effective Listening: Often overlooked, listening is a skill that can give you an edge in sales meetings.

- **Daily Task**: Practice active listening in every interaction by summarizing the other person's point of view to ensure understanding.
- **Detailed Explanation**: In sales meetings, this technique ensures you're addressing the client's actual needs and concerns, leading to more tailored solutions.

Real-Life Examples and Technique Exploration

Oprah Winfrey's Empathy: Oprah is renowned for her ability to deeply connect with people, a skill that she translates into her business endeavors.

- **Real-Life Anecdote**: Oprah's interviews showcase her ability to listen, empathize, and create a space where the other person feels valued, which is also a key element in successful sales meetings.

- **Training Recommendation**: Watch interviews conducted by Oprah and analyze her listening techniques and how she builds rapport.

Elon Musk's Product Knowledge: Elon Musk's presentations are grounded in deep product knowledge, which he communicates with clarity.

- **Real-Life Anecdote**: During Tesla's product launches, Musk's detailed explanations about the technology's features and benefits demonstrate his expertise, instilling confidence in his audience.

- **Training Recommendation**: Take complex information about your product and practice explaining it in simple, engaging terms.

Food for Thought: Reflect on a time when you were the customer. What made you trust the seller? How can you replicate that feeling of trust and assurance in your sales meetings?

Summary: Key Takeaways

1. Tailoring your value proposition to the client's unique needs can significantly enhance the relevance of your

pitch.

2. Building credibility is a daily practice that involves sharing your knowledge and insights generously.

3. Active listening is a skill that, when mastered, can provide a competitive advantage in understanding and addressing client needs more effectively.

4. Observing professionals like Oprah Winfrey and Elon Musk can provide insights into effective communication and product knowledge conveyance.

This section has been enriched with actionable strategies that a salesperson can adopt to make their sales meetings more effective. The tasks are designed to be integrated into the daily routine, ensuring steady progress and skill development over time.

The inclusion of real-life anecdotes about Oprah Winfrey and Elon Musk serves to demonstrate how these strategies play out successfully in various contexts. By examining their techniques, sales professionals can glean practical tips on empathy, product knowledge, and communication that they can then apply to their own sales meetings.

These strategies are not just techniques but foundational elements that shape the approach to sales, emphasizing preparation, personalized communication, and the importance of building trust. The food for thought encourages self-reflection, further grounding the concepts in personal experience, which is vital for understanding and connecting with clients on a deeper level. The summary consolidates the key points, offering a clear and concise reference to the core principles discussed in this section.

Food for Thought: The Confident Mindset

Consider this: Confidence is not the absence of fear; it's the mastery of it. How can you turn your inner doubts into fuel for a more compelling presentation?

Summary: Key Takeaways for Confident Sales Meetings

- **Psychological readiness**: This is the cornerstone of confidence.

- **Personal presentation**: How you present yourself physically can significantly affect your mental state and vice versa.

- **Engagement**: Remember, a sales meeting is a two-way conversation.

- **Agility**: The ability to pivot strategies mid-meeting is a sign of a confident and experienced salesperson.

Homework:

1. **Mock Meetings**: Schedule weekly mock sales meetings with a variety of scenarios.

2. **Feedback Collection**: After each real sales meeting, write down what went well and what could be improved.

3. **Confidence Journal**: Keep a journal of your sales meetings, noting instances where you felt confident and why.

Further Reading:

- "The Art of Closing the Sale" by Brian Tracy, for strategies on how to close with confidence.

- "Emotional Intelligence for Sales Success" by Colleen Stanley, to enhance your interpersonal skills for better sales outcomes.

In conclusion, handling sales meetings with confidence is not an innate talent but a skill built through preparation, practice, and self-reflection. By emulating the strategies of sales legends and adhering to a disciplined training regimen, you can enter any meeting room knowing that you're not just selling a product— you're offering a gateway to a solution, and doing so with the utmost conviction.

This outline provides a solid foundation for Chapter 15. To fulfill the requirements of the book, you would continue to elaborate on each section, including more real-life anecdotes, detailing the strategies more precisely, and expanding upon the training and daily tasks. Remember to interweave narratives and actionable advice to create an engaging and informative chapter that will stand out to any reader looking to improve their sales meeting acumen.

Chapter 16:

The Art of Following Up

In the labyrinth of sales processes, the follow-up is the thread that leads you back to the potential customer, allowing you to navigate the complexities of building a lasting relationship. It's where opportunities are nurtured and where the seeds of trust blossom into the fruits of partnership.

The Tale of a Persistent Salesman

Consider the tale of Colonel Harland Sanders, the founder of Kentucky Fried Chicken. He famously pitched his chicken recipe to over a thousand restaurants before finally securing a partnership. Sanders' story is not one of chance but of tenacity and the art of following up.

Understanding the Importance of Follow-Up

Deepened Strategy Explanations

Following up is not merely a courtesy; it is an essential step in the sales process that can distinguish a successful salesperson from the rest. Here's an expansion of the strategies that lead to effective follow-up:

Consistency and Timing: Following up at the right time and with consistent messages is key to staying top-of-mind with your clients.

- **Daily Task**: Create a follow-up calendar for each prospect that aligns with their buying cycles and your interaction history.
- **Detailed Explanation**: Timing your follow-ups can coincide with business cycles, industry events, or after the delivery of a new piece of value, such as a relevant article or case study.

Personalization: A follow-up that demonstrates personal attention to the client's specific situation and needs will always stand out.

- **Daily Task**: Customize each follow-up message by referencing previous discussions, current events in the client's industry, or shared experiences.
- **Detailed Explanation**: Personalization shows that you're not just sending a generic message, but that you're invested in a relationship with the client.

Adding Continuous Value: Each follow-up is an opportunity to add value to the client's life or business, reinforcing the benefits of your relationship.

- **Daily Task**: Identify a piece of information, a resource, or a contact that could benefit your client and include it in your follow-up.

- **Detailed Explanation**: This could be insights from a recent report, an introduction to a useful contact, or an invitation to an exclusive event.

Real-Life Examples and Technique Exploration

Steve Jobs' Product Follow-Up: Steve Jobs was known for his relentless follow-up on product details, which ensured Apple's products met his high standards.

- **Real-Life Anecdote**: Jobs would often call his team at odd hours to discuss product features or design elements, embodying the idea that follow-up is an ongoing, integral part of the process.
- **Training Recommendation**: Apply this same meticulousness to your follow-up strategy. Post-meeting, review your notes and identify three key points that would be most relevant to revisit with the client.

Jeff Bezos' Customer Obsession: Amazon's customer-centric approach is legendary, with follow-up playing a key role in understanding and meeting customer needs.

- **Real-Life Anecdote**: Bezos is known for attending to customer emails personally, even forwarding them to the relevant teams with a single character: "?", signaling the need for prompt follow-up and action.
- **Training Recommendation**: Incorporate direct customer feedback into your follow-ups. When a client mentions a challenge or a need, address it in your next communication.

Food for Thought: Think about a time when someone followed up with you in a manner that felt genuinely personalized. How did it make you feel, and how did it influence your perception of them or their company?

Summary: Key Takeaways

1. The timing of your follow-up can be as crucial as the content of the follow-up itself.

2. Personalization in follow-up communications shows attentiveness and commitment to the client's unique needs.

3. Adding value with each follow-up nurtures the relationship and can separate you from competitors who may not be as diligent.

4. Learning from industry leaders like Steve Jobs and Jeff Bezos can offer valuable insights into the discipline of follow-up and customer engagement.

This section has been enhanced to underscore the strategic significance of follow-up in the sales process. By incorporating these expanded strategies into daily routines, sales professionals can establish a more impactful presence in their prospects' minds, leading to stronger relationships and potentially more sales.

The section draws from the practices of renowned figures like Steve Jobs and Jeff Bezos to showcase how relentless follow-up and customer focus can create exceptional outcomes. The daily tasks and training recommendations are crafted to develop habits that can lead to consistent, personalized, and value-added communication.

These strategies go beyond just making a sale; they are about cultivating a long-term partnership with the client. The food for thought segment encourages self-reflection, which is crucial for empathizing with clients and improving one's follow-up methods. The summary acts as a concise reminder of the essential aspects of effective follow-up, aiding in retention and application of the concepts covered.

Daily Tasks and Training Program

Developing effective follow-up habits requires a disciplined approach:

1. **Daily Check-Ins**: Schedule a time each day dedicated solely to following up with prospects.
2. **CRM Mastery**: Become adept at using Customer Relationship Management tools to keep track of follow-up timelines.
3. **Communication Drills**: Role-play scenarios to practice follow-up calls, emails, and in-person visits.
4. **Feedback Analysis**: Regularly review responses from follow-ups to adjust your approach.

Actionable Strategies for Masterful Follow-Ups

- **Timeliness**: Follow up promptly according to the timeline you promised during your last interaction.
- **Personalization**: Tailor each follow-up to the prospect's specific needs and previous conversations.
- **Added Value**: Bring new insights or additional value to each follow-up to reinforce your commitment.
- **Persistence**: Don't mistake silence for disinterest. Be persistent but respectful.

Food for Thought: The Persistence-Perception Balance

Reflect on this: How can you balance persistence with perception? At what point does persistence become a nuisance, and how can you ensure your follow-ups are always perceived as valuable?

Summary: Key Takeaways for Effective Follow-Ups

- **Consistency is crucial**: Regular, predictable follow-ups create a rhythm of reliability.
- **Record Keeping**: Detailed notes of previous interactions can make follow-ups more effective and personal.
- **Multi-Channel Approach**: Use a combination of phone calls, emails, and social media to follow up, each with its strategic timing.

Homework:

1. **Follow-Up Calendar**: Create a follow-up calendar that schedules all follow-up activities.
2. **Prospect Profiles**: Develop comprehensive profiles for each prospect to inform your follow-up strategy.
3. **Scenario Planning**: Write scripts for different follow-up scenarios based on potential prospect responses.

Further Reading:

- "The Sales Follow-Up Handbook" by John L. Treace, for tips on how to stay in front of your customers without annoying them.
- "Follow Up and Close the Sale" by Jeff Shore, for insight into turning follow-ups into closed deals.

Chapter 17:

Closing Techniques That Work

Closing a sale is often envisioned as the grand finale of a theatrical performance; it's the climactic moment where all the earlier acts come together to deliver a satisfying conclusion. Mastering the close is both an art and a science, requiring a blend of psychology, timing, and strategy. This chapter uncovers the secrets behind effective closing techniques that can be applied across a range of sales scenarios.

The Story of the Big Close

Real-life anecdotes about closing sales often reveal the human element behind the strategies. Take the legendary tale of Joe Girard, recognized by the Guinness Book of World Records as the world's greatest salesman. He sold 13,001 cars at a Chevrolet dealership between 1963 and 1978, not by being pushy, but by creating an atmosphere where the close was a natural outcome of the conversation.

Understanding the Psychology of the Close

Closing a sale is as much an art as it is a science, engaging with the psychological processes that guide decision-making in buyers. To effectively close, one must not only present the offer but also align it with the emotional and logical processes of the customer.

Deepened Strategy Explanations

1. Creating a Sense of Urgency: Understanding the psychological impact of urgency is essential. It taps into the fear of missing out (FOMO) and can drive the buyer to act to avoid potential loss.

- **Daily Task**: Frame your conversations around time-sensitive opportunities or limited availability.
- **Detailed Explanation**: Explain the tangible losses or gains from acting now versus later, and use real-time data or case studies to back up your claims.

2. Leveraging Commitment and Consistency: People have a deep-seated need to be seen as consistent. Once someone verbally commits to something, they are more likely to go through with it.

- **Daily Task**: Encourage small commitments early in the sales process that can lead to the final close.
- **Detailed Explanation**: Use trial closes or statements that get the customer to agree with you on smaller points building up to the final ask.

Real-Life Examples and Technique Exploration

The Oprah Effect: Oprah Winfrey's endorsement of products often led to instant sell-outs. She understood the psychology of her audience and framed her endorsements to create immediate desire and action.

- **Real-Life Anecdote**: When Oprah mentioned her favorite things, she didn't just list them; she shared stories and her personal connection to them, engaging viewers emotionally and spurring them to action.

- **Training Recommendation**: Share personal stories or testimonials that connect with your product's benefits, thus leading the customer to close.

Elon Musk's Visionary Close: Elon Musk often closes on the vision of the future. He doesn't just sell a product; he sells an aspiration, a better future that customers want to be a part of.

- **Real-Life Anecdote**: Musk's presentation of Tesla's Roadster wasn't just about a car; it was about being part of the sustainable energy movement.

- **Training Recommendation**: Craft your closing pitch to include how the product or service fits into the grander vision or purpose that resonates with the buyer.

Food for Thought: How do you feel when you make a purchase? Are you seeking to fulfill a need, achieve consistency, or be part of something larger?

Summary: Key Takeaways

1. Urgency can compel action, but it must be genuine and not manipulative.

2. Small commitments can lead to larger ones. Use this knowledge to guide the customer through the sales process gently.

3. The psychological aspect of closing is about connection—connecting the product to the buyer's needs, desires, and aspirations.

4. Examining successful closes by figures like Oprah and Musk can offer invaluable insights into how to align your closing strategies with psychological triggers.

This section delves into the psychological elements that are crucial during the closing phase of a sale. By understanding and tapping into the emotional and logical decision-making processes of customers, sales professionals can craft a more effective closing strategy.

Drawing upon the techniques of influential personalities like Oprah Winfrey and Elon Musk serves to illustrate the power of emotional storytelling and visionary thinking in the art of the close. The daily tasks and training recommendations are designed to incorporate these strategies into a salesperson's routine, thereby building a natural progression towards the final commitment.

Understanding the psychological drivers behind purchasing decisions can empower sales professionals to create more resonant closing arguments and significantly increase their success rates. The summary reinforces the importance of these psychological strategies, ensuring they remain top-of-mind for the reader.

Daily Tasks and Training Program

1. **Role-Playing Exercises**: Daily sessions where you practice various closing scenarios with a colleague or a coach.

2. **Studying the Masters**: Dedicate time each day to study closing techniques from top sales professionals.

3. **Review and Reflect**: End each day by reviewing

your sales interactions and identifying what closing techniques worked or did not work.

Closing a sale is crucial, and choosing the right technique can make all the difference. Here are 20 effective closing techniques with detailed explanations:

Assumptive Close: Assume the sale is already made and talk about the next steps. This can psychologically encourage the customer to proceed because they envision themselves moving forward.

Now or Never Close: This is when you make the offer irresistible for a limited time, adding urgency to the purchase decision. "If you purchase today, you'll get an additional 15% off."

Summary Close: Summarize all the benefits and features agreed upon during the sales conversation, reinforcing the value and leading to a natural close.

Sharp Angle Close: When the customer asks for something extra, agree but only if they commit to the purchase right now. This can expedite the decision-making process.

Question Close: End the conversation with a question that leads to a positive outcome, such as, "Does this solution meet all the requirements we discussed?"

Takeaway Close: Suggest that perhaps the product may be too much for the customer's needs, causing them to reaffirm their interest.

Soft Close: Propose a non-threatening, low-commitment next step that leads them closer to the actual purchase. "Would you like to see how it looks in your space before deciding?"

Choice Close: Offer the prospect a choice between two options, both of which result in a sale. "Would you prefer the red one or the blue one?"

Ben Franklin Close: List the pros and cons with the prospect, usually demonstrating that the pros outweigh the cons.

Puppy Dog Close: Let the customer take the product home or try the service with no obligation, betting on them getting attached to it.

Balance Sheet Close: Draw a literal or figurative line down the middle of a page, listing the reasons for buying on one side and the reasons against on the other, helping them see the value outweighs the cost.

Trial Close: Check in with the prospect on a key point of agreement with a minor question, which does not ask for a final decision on the purchase.

Narrative Close: Tell a story of another customer who had similar needs and how your product or service provided the solution they were looking for.

The Columbo Close: As you're seemingly ending the conversation, you do a "Columbo" by asking a key question or revealing new information that can close the sale. "One more thing, if you decide today, I can offer you free installation."

Thermometer Close: Ask prospects to rate their interest on a scale of 1 to 10. Whatever they answer, you ask what it would take to move them up to a 10, and solve those concerns.

Cost of Delay Close: Emphasize the cost, loss, or disadvantage of not purchasing immediately.

Testimonial Close: Use a credible and relatable success story or testimonial to bolster the prospect's confidence in the product or service.

The Backwards Close: Start by discussing the post-purchase process, which gets the prospect thinking past the close and envisioning using the product or service.

The Best Time Close: Explain why there will never be a better time to buy than now, perhaps due to an impending price increase or diminishing availability.

The Consultative Close: This approach involves acting more as a consultant than a salesperson by recommending the best choice for them based on the discussion, which may naturally lead them to purchase.

Food for Thought: The Ethical Dilemma

Reflect on the importance of closing with integrity. How do you ensure that your techniques are not manipulative but are instead providing genuine value to the customer?

Summary: Key Takeaways for Effective Closing

- **Know Your Customer**: Tailor your closing technique to the customer's unique needs and desires.

- **Timing Is Everything**: Recognize when a customer is ready to close, and don't rush or delay.

- **Practice Makes Perfect**: Regularly refine your closing techniques through practice and real-world application.

Homework:

1. **Scenario Crafting**: Create detailed scenarios of different sales environments and practice closing techniques tailored to each.

2. **Closing Journal**: Keep a journal of your closing attempts, successes, and failures to refine your approach.

3. **Feedback Loop**: Solicit feedback from peers and mentors on your closing technique and integrate their advice.

Chapter 18:

The Digital Sales Landscape

The digital age has revolutionized the way we sell. It's not just about cold calls and face-to-face meetings anymore; it's about social media presence, online branding, and virtual pitches. This chapter will take you on a journey through the digital sales landscape, providing you with the strategies, anecdotes, and daily tasks that will prepare you to sell anything to anyone, anytime – and do it quickly and effectively online.

Anecdote: The Rise of a Digital Sales Leader

Let's start with a story about Sarah, a mid-level sales associate at a software company. Her turning point came when she decided to embrace digital tools fully. She diligently studied her company's CRM software, mastered email marketing campaigns, and used social media analytics to identify leads. Her efforts paid off when she landed a huge contract after a successful LinkedIn outreach campaign, catapulting her to the top of the sales leaderboard.

Famous Reference: Jeff Bezos' Digital Dominance

Jeff Bezos, the founder of Amazon, understood the power of the digital landscape before many others. He took a small online bookstore and turned it into one of the world's most powerful digital sales platforms. Bezos' relentless focus on customer experience, logistics, and innovative technology like AI-driven recommendations has made Amazon the epitome of digital sales success.

Understanding the Digital Landscape

The digital landscape is vast. It includes:

- E-commerce platforms
- Social media
- Email marketing
- Search engine optimization (SEO)
- Pay-per-click advertising (PPC)
- Content marketing
- Customer relationship management (CRM) systems

To thrive in digital sales, you need to understand how these elements work together to create a cohesive selling strategy.

Daily Tasks and Training Program

To master digital sales, commit to these daily tasks:

1. **Monitor Social Media Trends**: Spend 30 minutes analyzing trends on platforms like LinkedIn, Twitter, and Facebook.
2. **SEO Training**: Dedicate at least one hour a week to

learning about SEO and how to make your product easily discoverable online.

3. **Content Creation**: Develop or curate relevant content daily to engage with your audience and establish your expertise.

4. **Email Marketing**: Craft personalized outreach emails to your prospects and learn how to analyze the data from your campaigns.

5. **CRM Management**: Update your CRM system daily with new leads, notes on customer interactions, and follow-up tasks.

Actionable Strategies

1. **Leverage Social Selling**: Use social media not just for posting, but for listening and engaging with potential customers. Join groups, participate in discussions, and share valuable content.

2. **Optimize Your Online Presence**: Ensure your website and social media profiles are professional, up-to-date, and optimized for search engines and lead generation.

3. **Utilize Email Automation**: Implement email automation for follow-ups, but personalize the first and last paragraphs to make each communication feel bespoke.

4. **Adopt CRM Solutions**: A robust CRM can help track customer interactions and sales progress. Use data to understand customer behavior and predict sales trends.

5. **Create Valuable Content**: Develop blogs, whitepapers, videos, and infographics that address customer pain points and position your product as a solution.

Food for Thought

Reflect on these questions to better understand your digital sales approach:

- How well do you understand your digital tools, and where can you improve?
- Are you effectively using data to inform your digital sales strategy?
- How can you make your online interactions more personal and less automated?

Summaries

To summarize, the digital sales landscape is about harnessing technology to understand and connect with your customers. Sarah's anecdote reminds us of the potential personal growth that comes with mastering digital tools. The story of Jeff Bezos illustrates the transformative power of a comprehensive digital strategy.

Your training program is designed to develop daily habits that build your digital sales skills. The actionable strategies offered in this chapter will help you execute a digital sales strategy that feels personal to each customer. As you reflect on the provided questions and work through the training program, you'll start to see a significant improvement in your ability to sell digitally.

Remember, the digital sales landscape is ever-evolving, and staying ahead means constantly learning and adapting. By embracing these changes and continuously refining your digital sales approach, you will be able to sell anything, to anyone, anytime – quickly and effectively.

Chapter 19:

Social Selling Mastery

In an era where everyone is connected, social selling – the art of using social media to find and engage with new prospects – is more than a buzzword; it's a fundamental shift in how we do business. This chapter will guide you through mastering social selling, transforming your online interactions into successful sales.

Real-Life Anecdote: From Hashtags to Handshakes

Meet Maria. She's a rising star in the world of real estate. Maria's savvy use of Instagram transformed her career. By sharing stories of her journey, connecting with her audience, and leveraging hashtags, Maria created a personal brand that resonates with her audience. Her posts aren't just property listings; they're glimpses into the lifestyle her clients dream of. This personal touch turns followers into leads, and leads into clients.

Famous Story: Gary Vaynerchuk – The Social Media Sommelier

Gary Vaynerchuk, a Belarusian-American entrepreneur, started by taking his family's wine business and using YouTube to offer wine reviews in a down-to-earth style. This authentic approach to social media drew in a vast audience and skyrocketed sales. Gary's story is a testament to the power of social selling when combined with authenticity and passion.

The Pillars of Social Selling

To excel in social selling, one must understand its four pillars:

1. **Establishing a Strong Personal Brand**: Your online presence is your digital handshake. It's how prospects get to know you.

2. **Finding the Right Prospects**: Using social media to identify and engage with potential customers.

3. **Providing Value**: Sharing content that educates, entertains, or solves problems, positioning yourself as a thought leader.

4. **Building Relationships**: Engaging in conversations, not just broadcasting messages. True connection leads to trust, and trust leads to sales.

Daily Tasks and Training Program

Your daily social selling regimen should include:

1. **Personal Branding**: Post something daily that reinforces your brand. This could be a blog post, a comment on a trend, or a piece of advice.

2. **Prospect Engagement**: Spend 30 minutes identifying potential customers by monitoring conversations and joining groups related to your field.

3. **Content Sharing**: Share or retweet one piece of relevant content from a thought leader in your

industry every day.

4. **Direct Engagement**: Send at least five personalized messages to new or existing contacts, offering insights or help, not selling.

5. **Feedback Analysis**: End your day by analyzing feedback and engagement from your posts to refine your strategy.

Actionable Strategies

1. **Optimize Your Profiles**: Make sure your social profiles are professional, with a clear value proposition and call to action.

2. **Listen and Engage**: Use social listening tools to monitor mentions of your brand, competitors, and industry keywords.

3. **Curate and Create**: Share a mix of curated content and original thought leadership pieces that showcase your expertise.

4. **Influence Through Interaction**: Comment on posts, answer questions, and participate in discussions to increase your visibility and influence.

5. **Measure Your Success**: Use analytics to track engagement and adjust your strategy accordingly.

Food for Thought

- How does your personal brand reflect your professional value?

- Are you genuinely engaging with your prospects, or just broadcasting?

- What types of content can you create or share to showcase your expertise?

Summaries

Social selling is more than just selling; it's about building a brand that people trust. Maria's success story exemplifies the power of personal branding on social media. Gary Vaynerchuk's transformation from a wine merchant to a social media mogul illustrates the potential of combining your passion with social media proficiency.

The daily tasks and training program outlined in this chapter will help you make social selling a habit. The actionable strategies give you a clear roadmap to engage with prospects genuinely and provide value, establishing yourself as a trusted advisor in your industry.

To master social selling, remember that it's about fostering relationships, not just pushing products. By following the guidance in this chapter, you'll be well on your way to social selling mastery, able to sell anything, to anyone, anytime – quickly and through the power of social connection.

Chapter 20:

Email Prospecting: Writing Emails That Get Responses

In the digital age, the power of a well-crafted email cannot be underestimated. Email prospecting, when done right, can open doors that seemed forever closed and create opportunities where none appeared to exist. This chapter is your guide to mastering the craft of email prospecting.

Real-Life Anecdote: David's Dilemma

David, a startup founder, was struggling to get responses from potential investors. After dozens of unanswered emails, he revised his approach, focusing on personalized, value-driven messages that spoke directly to the investors' interests. The result? A reply rate that went from virtually zero to over 40%, and eventually, the funding he needed.

Famous Story: J.K. Rowling's Rejection Letters

Before J.K. Rowling became a household name with the Harry Potter series, she faced multiple rejections. Her pitches were often ignored or dismissed. Yet, she refined her approach with each email, making her proposal more compelling. Her persistence and ability to communicate her novel's potential eventually led to her breakthrough success.

The Craft of Email Prospecting

The art of email prospecting revolves around several key principles:

1. **Clarity of Purpose**: Be clear about what you want the recipient to do after reading your email.

2. **Brevity and Directness**: Keep it short and sweet. Time is precious, and a concise email respects that.

3. **Personalization**: Show that you've done your homework and that you're reaching out to them specifically, not just sending a mass email.

4. **Value Proposition**: Quickly articulate what's in it for them, not just for you.

5. **Call to Action**: Be specific about the next steps you want the recipient to take.

Daily Tasks and Training Program

1. **Research and Personalize**: Dedicate time each morning to researching your prospects to tailor your emails.

2. **Write and Revise**: Craft your emails carefully, then take a break and revisit them for revisions.

3. **Follow-up Sequence**: Plan and schedule a sequence of follow-up emails for those who don't respond initially.

4. **Analyze Responses**: Review any responses you get to understand what worked and what didn't.

5. **Continuous Learning**: Spend time each day reading about successful email strategies and incorporating new techniques into your approach.

Actionable Strategies

1. **Subject Line Success**: Use engaging and clear subject lines. Think about what would make you want to open an email.

2. **First Line Impact**: Make your opening line about them, not you. Grab their attention by mentioning a recent achievement of theirs or a mutual connection.

3. **Social Proof**: Include a sentence about who you've worked with or results you've achieved that are relevant to the prospect.

4. **Clear Call to Action**: Don't leave them wondering what to do next. If you want a meeting, ask for it. If you want feedback, be specific.

5. **Timing and Technology**: Utilize email tracking tools to understand the best times to send emails and when your emails are being opened.

Food for Thought

- How can you apply the principles of persuasive writing to your email prospecting?

- In what ways can you demonstrate that you understand your prospect's challenges and goals?

- What can you offer that is of genuine value to your prospects?

Summaries

Effective email prospecting is a blend of art and science. David's story illustrates the importance of personalization and persistence, while J.K. Rowling's initial rejections underscore the necessity of resilience and the power of a compelling message.

The daily tasks and training program are designed to integrate best practices into your routine, making the process of crafting powerful emails second nature. By employing the actionable strategies laid out in this chapter, your emails will stand out in a crowded inbox.

Remember, the goal of email prospecting is not just to get a response but to start a conversation that leads to a mutually beneficial relationship. With the guidance provided here, you will be well-equipped to write emails that not only get responses but also build the foundations of successful sales.

Chapter 21:

Negotiating Win-Win Solutions

Negotiation is the art of finding the golden middle path, a harmonious agreement where all parties feel they've gained. It's not about conquering the other side, but rather, about collaborating to achieve a result that everyone can be satisfied with. This chapter will guide you through the process of creating win-win solutions, ensuring that you come out of negotiations not just with a deal, but with a partnership strengthened and ready for future growth.

Real-Life Anecdote: Maya's Market Standoff

Maya, a procurement manager, faced a tough negotiation with a key supplier. Prices were rising, and her company was struggling to keep costs down. Instead of making demands, Maya invited the supplier to discuss how they could overcome this challenge together. The result was an agreement that provided her company with better prices in exchange for a longer contract term, giving the supplier more stability.

Famous Story: The Disney-Pixar Deal

The negotiation between Disney and Pixar serves as an iconic example of a win-win solution. In 2006, Disney bought Pixar, but instead of a takeover, they framed it as a partnership. Ed Catmull and John Lasseter of Pixar were given leadership of Disney's animation department, ensuring Pixar's culture remained intact. This led to a renaissance in Disney animation, with hits like 'Frozen' and 'Tangled', proving that the right deal can lead to thriving success for all involved.

Understanding Negotiation Dynamics

Negotiation is not just a business interaction; it's a human interaction. Here's what you need to keep in mind:

1. **Interests vs. Positions**: Focus on the underlying interests, not just the stated positions.
2. **Creative Problem Solving**: Think outside the box to find solutions that fulfill the interests of both parties.
3. **Relationship Building**: Remember that the relationship is just as important as the deal itself.
4. **Effective Communication**: Listen actively and articulate your points clearly and persuasively.
5. **Emotional Intelligence**: Be aware of emotions—yours and theirs—and manage them effectively.

Daily Tasks and Training Program

1. **Skill Building**: Start each day with a negotiation exercise, such as role-playing scenarios.
2. **Market Research**: Keep abreast of market trends and pricing information to inform your negotiation strategy.

3. **Relationship Maintenance**: Allocate time daily to build and maintain relationships with key partners.

4. **Self-Reflection**: At the end of each day, reflect on a negotiation you've observed or participated in and identify what worked and what didn't.

5. **Continuous Education**: Dedicate time weekly to study negotiation tactics and strategies.

Actionable Strategies

1. **BATNA Identification**: Before any negotiation, determine your Best Alternative to a Negotiated Agreement to understand your leverage.

2. **Mutual Gains Approach**: Aim to find options that offer gains to both sides.

3. **Strategic Concessions**: Plan what you can concede and when, ensuring that for any concession you make, you get one in return.

4. **The Power of Pause**: Don't be afraid to pause the negotiation to avoid reactive decisions.

5. **Finalizing Deals**: Always end negotiations with a clear summary of agreed terms and next steps.

Food for Thought

- Reflect on a time when you achieved a win-win outcome. What strategies helped you succeed?

- Consider a negotiation that did not go as planned. What could you have done differently?

- How can you make sure the relationship is enhanced, not hurt, by the negotiation process?

Summaries

Negotiation is a subtle dance that requires patience, empathy, and strategic thinking. Maya's approach in the market standoff exemplifies the importance of mutual respect and understanding, while the Disney-Pixar deal showcases the heights that can be reached when both parties are invested in each other's success.

The daily tasks and training program are aimed at building your negotiation muscles, making you a more formidable, yet fair, negotiator. The strategies outlined are your toolbox for navigating these complex interactions.

In summary, remember that the best deals are the ones where no one feels like they've lost, where every party walks away ready to work together again. With this mindset and the skills you've developed, you are well on your way to negotiating not just deals, but lasting partnerships and paths to shared success.

Sales Metrics Dashboard to Measure Success Rate

Chapter 22:

Sales Metrics and KPIs

In the world of sales, knowledge is power. Sales metrics and Key Performance Indicators (KPIs) are the compass and map that guide sales professionals toward success, providing the insight needed to navigate the competitive landscape.

The Tale of Two Sales Teams: An Anecdote

Consider the story of two sales teams within the same company – Team A was led by intuitive decision-making, while Team B drove every strategy based on data. Over time, Team B consistently outperformed their counterparts by adapting to real-time metrics, showcasing the undeniable power of data-driven sales strategies.

A Famous Example: The Oracle of Omaha

Warren Buffett, known for his investing prowess, makes financial decisions based on hard data and clear metrics.

His approach mirrors the disciplined, metric-focused strategies essential in sales. Buffett's success underlines the importance of informed decision-making in any business context.

Understanding Sales Metrics and KPIs

1. **Sales Volume**: The total units sold or total revenue in a given period.

2. **Conversion Rate**: The percentage of prospects who turn into customers.

3. **Average Deal Size**: The average revenue per closed deal.

4. **Sales Cycle Length**: The average time it takes to close a deal.

5. **Customer Acquisition Cost (CAC)**: The total cost of acquiring a new customer.

6. **Customer Lifetime Value (CLV)**: The total revenue a business can expect from a single customer account.

7. **Churn Rate**: The rate at which customers stop doing business with an entity.

Daily Tasks and Training Program

1. **Data Analysis**: Begin each day by reviewing the previous day's sales data to identify trends and areas for improvement.

2. **Goal Setting**: Set daily, weekly, and monthly targets based on historical data and trend analysis.

3. **Training Sessions**: Conduct regular training on interpreting data and using CRM tools effectively.

4. **Role-Playing**: Use role-playing exercises to practice handling different sales scenarios based on metric predictions.

5. **Continuous Learning**: Dedicate time to staying updated on new metrics and analytical tools that can improve sales processes.

Actionable Strategies

1. **Monitor Real-Time Data**: Use CRM tools to monitor sales activities in real-time and adjust tactics accordingly.

2. **Segment and Target**: Analyze metrics to segment customers effectively and tailor sales strategies to different groups.

3. **Invest in Technology**: Utilize advanced analytics and AI tools to gain deeper insights into sales trends.

4. **Enhance Training**: Regularly update sales training to include the latest best practices in data analysis and metric utilization.

5. **Benchmarking**: Regularly compare your metrics against industry standards to gauge performance.

Food for Thought

- How can you incorporate sales metrics into your daily decision-making process more effectively?

- Reflect on a time when ignoring the data led to a missed opportunity. What lesson did you learn?

- In what ways can you ensure that the data you collect is as accurate and helpful as possible?

Summaries

The narratives of Team B and Warren Buffett provide compelling evidence of the efficacy of a metrics-driven approach in sales. Understanding and effectively utilizing sales metrics and KPIs can significantly enhance your sales strategies and outcomes.

The daily tasks and training reinforce the importance of a disciplined approach to data. By continuously measuring performance against clear KPIs, sales professionals can refine their strategies, ensuring they stay on the path to success.

In conclusion, sales metrics and KPIs are the foundation of a modern, effective sales strategy. By mastering these tools, sales professionals can predict trends, adapt to changes, and achieve consistent growth. Remember, in sales, the best decisions are always informed by data.

Chapter 23:

Using CRM Systems for
Sales Success

Introduction: In the realm of sales, Customer Relationship Management (CRM) systems are not just tools; they are the pivot points around which successful sales strategies revolve. The power of CRM systems lies in their ability to organize customer data, streamline processes, and enhance communication.

Anecdote: The Transformation of Sprockets Inc. Consider the story of Sprockets Inc., a mid-sized company struggling to keep its customer data organized. Lost information, missed follow-ups, and chaotic sales meetings were daily occurrences until they implemented a CRM system. Within a quarter, their sales productivity skyrocketed, customer satisfaction scores improved, and revenues increased by 30%.

A Nod to the Famous: Salesforce's Marc Benioff Marc Benioff, the founder of Salesforce, didn't just build a company; he revolutionized the concept of CRM. He understood that the future of sales was in cloud-based CRM systems that could manage customer information effectively and be accessible from anywhere, at any time.

The Essentials of CRM:

- **Contact Management**: A CRM system's core, enabling the storage of customer information in an organized manner.
- **Sales Automation**: Streamlining repetitive tasks to increase efficiency.
- **Interaction Tracking**: Keeping a log of all communications with prospects and customers.
- **Lead Management**: Tracking potential customers through the sales pipeline.
- **Reporting and Dashboards**: Visual representations of sales data and metrics.

Daily Tasks and Training Program:

1. **Data Entry Discipline**: Train sales staff on the importance of recording every customer interaction in the CRM.
2. **Daily Review Routines**: Begin each day by reviewing the scheduled tasks and follow-ups in the CRM.
3. **Weekly CRM Workshops**: Host workshops to explore advanced CRM features that may enhance productivity.
4. **Monthly Data Cleaning**: Dedicate time each month for database maintenance to ensure data integrity.
5. **Role-Based Access Control**: Ensure each team member understands their level of access and how to use the

CRM in their role.

Actionable Strategies

In today's sales landscape, harnessing the power of technology, particularly Customer Relationship Management (CRM) systems, can provide a competitive edge. Here we explore actionable strategies to make CRM an invaluable ally in the art of selling.

1. Segmentation for Personalization

Deepening Strategy Explanations:

- **Strategy**: CRM data allows for precise market segmentation, leading to highly personalized marketing and sales campaigns which resonate on an individual level.
- **Daily Task**: Review customer data daily to identify patterns and create new segments.
- **Training Program**: Regular workshops on data analytics and segment marketing.

Real-Life Example:

- **Anecdote**: Netflix's recommendation system is a prime example of segmentation and personalization. By analyzing user data, Netflix personalizes suggestions, resulting in increased viewer engagement.
- **Famous Relate**: Amazon's Jeff Bezos emphasizes the use of data for personalization, driving Amazon's recommendations engine, which contributes significantly to their sales.

2. Sales Forecasting

Deepening Strategy Explanations:

- **Strategy**: Use CRM forecasting tools to anticipate market trends and prepare for future demand.
- **Daily Task**: Input all customer interactions into the CRM to enhance forecasting accuracy.
- **Training Program**: Monthly forecasting analysis sessions to interpret CRM data and adjust sales tactics.

Real-Life Example:

- **Anecdote**: A tech company accurately forecasted a surge in demand for remote work tools by analyzing CRM data trends during the early stages of the global shift to remote work.
- **Famous Relate**: Warren Buffett's investment strategy, although not directly linked to CRM, emphasizes the importance of forecasting and understanding market trends for strategic decision-making.

3. Customer Feedback Loop

Deepening Strategy Explanations:

- **Strategy**: Incorporate customer feedback directly into the CRM to ensure sales strategies remain customer-centric.
- **Daily Task**: After each customer interaction, record feedback and make it a point to follow up on the input provided.
- **Training Program**: Bi-weekly training on effective feedback collection and analysis.

Real-Life Example:

- **Anecdote**: A lifestyle brand used CRM-integrated customer feedback to refine its product line, resulting in a 25% increase in customer satisfaction.
- **Famous Relate**: Apple, under Steve Jobs, was notorious for valuing customer experience, often iterating products based on user feedback.

4. Automated Reporting

Deepening Strategy Explanations:

- **Strategy**: Leverage automated CRM reporting to have real-time access to sales performance data.
- **Daily Task**: Check automated reports every morning to gauge the previous day's sales performance.
- **Training Program**: Quarterly training on interpreting automated reports and actionable insights.

Real-Life Example:

- **Anecdote**: A SaaS company implemented automated CRM reporting which allowed them to quickly adapt to market changes, outpacing competitors.
- **Famous Relate**: Salesforce CEO Marc Benioff champions the use of real-time analytics for dynamic business maneuvering.

5. Mobile CRM

Deepening Strategy Explanations:

- **Strategy**: Provide sales teams with mobile CRM access to enable timely updates and communication.

- **Daily Task**: Encourage sales reps to update CRM entries immediately after each meeting or sales call.
- **Training Program**: Implement a 'mobile-first' training module focusing on efficient CRM usage on mobile devices.

Real-Life Example:

- **Anecdote**: A real estate agency increased their closing rate by 18% after providing agents with mobile CRM access, enabling them to respond to clients promptly.
- **Famous Relate**: LinkedIn's Reid Hoffman believes in the power of connectivity; mobile CRM embodies this by allowing sales professionals to connect with their network and data anywhere.

Food for Thought: Consider how the integration of technology in your sales process can not only streamline operations but also bring a level of personalization and responsiveness that today's customers expect.

Summary: Key Takeaways

1. Personalization through segmentation can transform the customer experience and drive sales.
2. Accurate sales forecasting allows for strategic planning and resource allocation.
3. A customer feedback loop is essential for continuous improvement and customer satisfaction.
4. Automated reporting provides the insights needed to make data-driven decisions.
5. Mobile CRM accessibility ensures sales teams can act

quickly, no matter where they are.

By deepening the understanding and application of these CRM strategies, sales teams can significantly improve their efficiency and effectiveness. The real-life examples and connections to successful figures in business provide inspiration and validation of these strategies, reinforcing the notion that CRM systems are not just about technology but about fostering better customer relationships and driving sales growth.

This enhanced section not only outlines the CRM strategies but ties them into daily practices and developmental programs, underlining their practical applications. Real-life anecdotes and examples from industry giants underscore the real-world effectiveness of these strategies. The section aims to bridge the gap between theoretical knowledge and actual implementation, encouraging a culture of continuous learning and adaptation in the fast-evolving sales landscape.

Food for Thought:

- Reflect on how a CRM system can not only be a repository of data but also a strategic advisor for your sales efforts.
- Consider the potential of integrating AI into your CRM system. How could it transform your sales processes?
- Contemplate the power of personalization in your CRM-driven sales strategy. How can you tailor your approach to individual customer needs more effectively?

Summary: CRM systems are indispensable in the modern sales landscape. As illustrated by Sprockets Inc.'s story and Marc

Benioff's vision, CRM platforms can be transformative when used effectively. This chapter has explored the features of CRM systems, their impact on daily sales activities, and strategic insights that can drive success.

Sales teams that harness the power of a CRM not only work smarter but also deliver better customer experiences and drive higher sales. As the sales world continues to evolve, the integration and intelligent use of CRM systems remain a vital component of a successful sales strategy.

Remember, a CRM system is more than software—it's the backbone of your customer relationships and sales success.

Chapter 24:

Time Management for Sales Professionals

Introduction: In the high-octane field of sales, time isn't just money—it's your most precious resource. How you manage your hours directly correlates with your success. Effective time management separates the best from the rest. This chapter will dissect the art of time management in sales, providing strategies that have been battle-tested in the field.

Anecdote: Jim's Leap to Top Performer Jim, a sales rep at a software company, felt he was always busy but not productive. His turning point came when he attended a time management workshop and realized the power of prioritizing tasks. By applying the techniques he learned, Jim transformed from an average performer to the top salesperson in his company within a year.

A Story of Legendary Proportions: The Wisdom of Warren Buffett Warren Buffett, one of the most successful investors and business magnates, once gave his pilot a simple yet powerful piece of advice about setting priorities, which is directly applicable to sales. He asked his pilot to list his top 25 career goals and then to circle the five most important. Buffett's insight was that the 20 not circled should be avoided at all costs as they distract from the critical goals—a principle that can be applied to sales tasks and priorities.

Mastering Time Management

Time management is arguably one of the most critical skills in the arsenal of a successful sales professional. Mastering it ensures that you're always focused on the right tasks at the right time, ultimately leading to increased productivity and sales.

Task Prioritization

Deepening Strategy Explanations:

- **Strategy**: Use the Eisenhower Matrix to distinguish between tasks that are urgent and important, important but not urgent, urgent but not important, and neither urgent nor important. This helps in prioritizing tasks that align with your sales goals.
- **Daily Task**: Begin your day by categorizing tasks into the Eisenhower Matrix and tackle them accordingly.
- **Training Program**: Hold quarterly time management workshops focusing on effective task prioritization.

Real-Life Example:

- **Anecdote**: A pharmaceutical sales rep reallocated their time to focus on high-prescribing doctors after using the Eisenhower Matrix, which led to a substantial increase in sales.

- **Famous Relate**: Dwight D. Eisenhower, the 34th President of the United States, developed the matrix that now bears his name, exemplifying its use through his accomplished military and political career.

The Pomodoro Technique

Deepening Strategy Explanations:

- **Strategy**: Work in focused sprints (Pomodoros) of 25 minutes followed by a 5-minute break to maintain high levels of concentration without burning out.
- **Daily Task**: Implement the Pomodoro Technique during the most productive hours of your day.
- **Training Program**: Incorporate Pomodoro sessions into daily sales activities and measure the impact on productivity.

Real-Life Example:

- **Anecdote**: A startup CEO adopted the Pomodoro Technique to manage their day and found they could complete tasks in two-thirds of the time it used to take.
- **Famous Relate**: Francesco Cirillo, who developed the Pomodoro Technique, showcases how it can be used to accomplish tasks with relentless focus.

Time Blocking

Deepening Strategy Explanations:

- **Strategy**: Dedicate specific time blocks for different tasks or activities, such as prospecting, follow-up calls, or client meetings, and adhere to these times as you would a client appointment.

- **Daily Task**: Schedule your day in blocks of time dedicated to specific sales activities.

- **Training Program**: Implement a training module on strategic planning, encouraging sales reps to use time blocking to manage their daily schedules.

Real-Life Example:

- **Anecdote**: A real estate agent managed to double their showings by strictly following a time-blocked schedule, leading to an increase in sales.

- **Famous Relate**: Elon Musk is known for his meticulous time-blocking, sometimes breaking his day into five-minute slots to maximize productivity.

Automation and Delegation

Deepening Strategy Explanations:

- **Strategy**: Identify repetitive tasks that can be automated with software and tasks that can be delegated to support staff. This frees up more time to focus on engaging with clients and closing sales.

- **Daily Task**: Review daily activities to identify opportunities for automation or delegation.

- **Training Program**: Regular training on new automation tools and delegation techniques to optimize sales processes.

Real-Life Example:

- **Anecdote**: By automating their lead generation process, a sales team was able to spend more time in direct communication with prospects, which led to a

30% increase in closed deals.

- **Famous Relate**: Richard Branson, the founder of the Virgin Group, is an advocate for delegation, often citing it as a key reason for his many successes across various industries.

Food for Thought: In sales, time is money. How you manage your hours directly correlates with your sales results. Reflect on your daily habits and ask yourself if they align with your highest priorities and sales targets.

Summary: Key Takeaways

1. Prioritization is crucial - focus on tasks that drive sales and delegate or delay less critical ones.
2. The Pomodoro Technique can help maintain focus and prevent burnout.
3. Time blocking ensures you're dedicating appropriate attention to key sales activities.
4. Embrace automation and delegation to free up your time for tasks that require your unique sales expertise.

These strategies are not only about working harder but working smarter. By refining your approach to time management, you create more opportunities to engage with clients, build relationships, and close deals. Embracing these methods and making them part of your daily routine can transform your productivity and effectiveness as a sales professional.

This section builds upon the fundamental strategies of time management by providing a deeper understanding of how they can be applied in a sales context. It includes a mix of daily tasks to reinforce discipline, training programs to develop skills, and anecdotes to demonstrate real-world application, all aiming to transform sales professionals into time management experts. Each strategy is framed to not only optimize time but also to enhance the overall sales process, underscoring the importance of strategic focus in achieving sales success.

Daily Tasks and Training Program:

1. **Morning Routine**: Start your day with a clear routine that includes reviewing your CRM for the day's priorities.

2. **Daily Planning**: Spend the first 15 minutes planning your day, aligning tasks with your sales targets.

3. **Focused Sales Blocks**: Dedicate uninterrupted blocks of time to prospecting, following up, and closing deals.

4. **Learning and Development**: End your day with a brief session devoted to skills development or market research.

Actionable Strategies:

1. **80/20 Rule**: Apply the Pareto Principle by focusing 80% of your time on the 20% of your clients or activities that generate the most sales.

2. **Time Audit**: Conduct weekly time audits to identify time-wasters and areas for improvement.

3. **Consistent Follow-up**: Schedule follow-ups diligently within your CRM to ensure no lead falls through the cracks.

4. **Batch Processing**: Group similar tasks together to increase efficiency and reduce context switching.

Food for Thought:

- Reflect on the activities that bring the most value to your sales process. Are you dedicating enough time to these activities?

- Consider how the discipline of time management can become your competitive advantage in the sales world.

- Ponder on the potential benefits of a balanced work-life rhythm for long-term sales success.

Summary: Time management in sales is about making intentional choices with how your time is spent. Jim's journey to sales stardom and Buffett's sage advice underscore the importance of prioritization and focus. Through meticulous planning, strategic task allocation, and continuous self-improvement, you can not only increase your sales but also enhance your overall job satisfaction.

The sales professionals who climb to the top are those who not only work hard but also work smart by managing their time with precision. By internalizing the strategies and mindsets discussed in this chapter, you are not just managing time— you're managing your pathway to sales excellence.

Chapter 25:

Building and Managing a Sales Team

Introduction: Behind every great product is an outstanding sales team propelling it forward. The right team can be the rocket fuel for a company's growth, turning potential into profits. This chapter dives into the nuances of building a robust sales team and the strategies for managing it effectively, ensuring your product isn't just another drop in the ocean of offerings.

The Foundation - A Story of Unlikely Success: Consider the story of Barbara Corcoran, real estate mogul and "Shark Tank" investor. She turned a $1,000 loan into a billion-dollar business by building a team that complemented her skills and compensated for her weaknesses. Her ability to choose the right people and inspire them to greatness was key to her success.

Key Elements in Building a Sales Team

Building a high-performing sales team is much like conducting an orchestra. Each member plays a different instrument, contributing to a harmonious performance, led by a conductor who knows how to bring out the best in each musician. In sales, the instruments are the diverse skills and personalities of your team, and the music they produce is the revenue they generate.

Identifying Talent

The identification of talent goes beyond examining a resume; it's about discerning potential and recognizing the traits that match your company's culture and sales goals.

- **Strategy Expansion**: Develop an 'Ideal Candidate Profile' that includes not just educational background and experience, but also soft skills like communication, adaptability, and resilience. Sales aptitude assessments can be invaluable tools here.
- **Case Study**: Look at Salesforce, a CRM giant. They don't just hire based on experience; they look for 'Ohana', which in Hawaiian culture represents family bonds. This principle is central to their hiring, seeking individuals who share their values of trust, customer success, innovation, and equality.

Diverse Skill Sets

Diversity in your team can be your greatest strength, offering a kaleidoscope of perspectives and approaches to problem-solving.

- **Strategy Expansion**: Evaluate the team's needs and seek individuals who fill specific gaps, whether it's industry experience, technical know-how, or a knack for nurturing client relationships.
- **Case Study**: IBM's sales team diversity is not just about culture or background; it's also about cognitive

diversity. They harness this by forming teams that think differently, bringing together veterans with newcomers to encourage mentorship and fresh ideas.

Structured Hiring Process

A standardized hiring process ensures you evaluate candidates consistently and fairly, while also giving candidates a clear understanding of their potential role and responsibilities.

- **Strategy Expansion**: Incorporate scenario-based evaluations that simulate sales challenges the candidates would face on the job. This helps in assessing how they would perform under real-world conditions.

- **Case Study**: HubSpot, an inbound marketing, sales, and service software provider, uses role-playing extensively in their hiring process. Candidates must demonstrate how they would handle various stages of the sales process, from prospecting to closing.

Training and Development

Continuous training is crucial. A salesperson's education is never complete; there are always new skills to learn, new products to understand, and new sales strategies to master.

- **Strategy Expansion**: Invest in a learning management system (LMS) where sales reps can access training material. Encourage ongoing learning through certifications and industry-related courses.

- **Case Study**: Xerox, known for its sales prowess, has an established university for sales professionals. Xerox focuses on continuous learning and has been renowned for producing some of the best-trained salespeople in the world.

Team Cohesion and Morale

Fostering a collaborative environment where salespeople can learn from one another and feel part of a team is essential for morale and retention.

- **Strategy Expansion**: Create team-building activities that are not solely about work. Include regular team outings or socials that help build trust and camaraderie.

- **Case Study**: Google's sales teams are known for their cohesion, often attributed to the company's culture that encourages 'Googliness' – a blend of fun, intellectual challenge, and teamwork.

Performance Monitoring and Feedback

Regular performance reviews, constructive feedback, and recognition are key to keeping a sales team motivated and on target.

- **Strategy Expansion**: Utilize Customer Relationship Management (CRM) tools to track performance metrics and provide data-driven feedback.

- **Case Study**: At Oracle, data-driven performance reviews are standard. By leveraging their robust CRM systems, sales managers provide specific, actionable feedback to their teams.

Compensation and Incentives

Competitive compensation and incentive programs are critical to attract and retain top sales talent.

- **Strategy Expansion**: Structure a transparent compensation plan with a mix of fixed salary, commissions, and bonuses tied to individual and team performance.
- **Case Study**: Zillow, a leading real estate marketplace, offers a clear and competitive compensation package that rewards both individual achievement and team collaboration, leading to higher motivation levels.

Summary: Key Takeaways

1. Identifying talent that fits your culture and goals is crucial for long-term success.
2. A diverse sales team with a mix of skills can address a broader range of customer needs.
3. A structured hiring process with role-playing can help identify candidates who will perform well in real-life scenarios.
4. Continuous training and development ensure your team stays competitive.
5. Team cohesion is vital for morale and can be built through both professional collaboration and social activities.
6. Performance should be monitored regularly, with feedback provided in a constructive manner.
7. Compensation and incentives need to be competitive and performance-based to retain top talent.

Food for Thought: Remember, building a successful sales team is a continuous process. It starts with hiring the right people, but it certainly doesn't end there.

The Daily Grind – Tasks and Training:

1. **Daily Huddles**: Start each day with a brief team meeting to set the tone, discuss goals, and share motivational insights.

2. **Ongoing Training**: Implement regular training sessions focused on both product knowledge and sales skills development.

3. **Performance Monitoring**: Use daily and weekly KPIs to measure individual and team performance, providing immediate feedback.

Anecdote - The Power of Motivation: Jim, a sales manager, noticed a dip in his team's performance. By introducing a "Salesperson of the Month" award, he saw a marked increase in productivity and morale, illustrating the impact of motivation.

Effective Sales Team Management

Creating a winning sales team is akin to a master chef bringing together a medley of ingredients to create a perfect dish. The ingredients, in this case, are the unique personalities and talents of your salespeople, and the dish is the collective success of your team.

Leadership Style

Leadership in sales is not a one-size-fits-all approach; it requires a blend of intuition, flexibility, and strategic thinking. The most effective sales leaders are those who can adapt their style to the needs of their team, while maintaining clear goals and expectations.

- **Strategy Expansion**: Practice situational leadership, adapting your approach based on the experience level of team members, the urgency of tasks, and the overall sales environment.

- **Case Study**: Satya Nadella's leadership at Microsoft has been transformative, focusing on a growth mindset. He shifted the culture from one of know-it-all to learn-it-all, leading to a significant increase in Microsoft's market value.

Communication

Open communication forms the bedrock of trust within a team. It involves not only the transmission of information but also active listening and the facilitation of a dialogue where every member feels heard and valued.

- **Strategy Expansion**: Implement regular one-on-one and team meetings that go beyond discussing sales targets. Use these opportunities to understand team members' career aspirations and personal goals.
- **Case Study**: Slack, the communication platform, uses its own tool to foster open and transparent communication within its teams. They create channels for specific topics, ensuring information is shared effectively and in real time.

Incentives and Rewards

Motivation varies between individuals; what inspires one person may not inspire another. Effective sales team management requires understanding these differences and crafting incentive programs that recognize and reward diverse achievements.

- **Strategy Expansion**: Develop a tiered incentive program that offers a combination of monetary and non-monetary rewards. Recognize both the results (e.g., sales volume) and the behaviors (e.g., teamwork, customer service) that lead to those results.

- **Case Study**: At Adobe, the sales team is incentivized through a program called 'Kickbox'. It gives employees freedom and funds to pursue their own ideas, encouraging innovation and ownership.

Managing Performance

Performance management is not just about hitting targets; it's about developing the skills and strategies that enable consistent achievement over time.

- **Strategy Expansion**: Use performance data to identify strengths and areas for improvement. Provide sales coaching that is tailored to each individual's needs and development plans.

- **Case Study**: Accenture shifted from annual performance reviews to a more fluid system. Managers give timely feedback using digital tools, aligning individual goals with business priorities and offering continuous, forward-looking career guidance.

Empowerment and Professional Development

Empowering your sales team means giving them the tools, authority, and responsibility to make decisions and act on them. This empowerment comes with an expectation of accountability but also fosters a sense of ownership over one's work.

- **Strategy Expansion**: Encourage salespeople to take the lead on projects and client relationships. Offer leadership development programs to those who show potential and interest in advancing their careers.

- **Case Study**: Google empowers its employees by fostering a culture of autonomy. The tech giant encourages its sales teams to spend time on projects they are passionate about, leading to innovations like AdWords and Gmail.

Building a Collaborative Culture

Collaboration within a sales team can lead to shared learning and more innovative approaches to reaching sales targets.

- **Strategy Expansion**: Create opportunities for team members to work together on projects, share insights, and celebrate each other's successes.
- **Case Study**: Atlassian, known for its team collaboration software like Trello and Jira, practices what they preach. They create collaborative work environments for their sales teams, which has contributed to a robust and loyal customer base.

Summary: Key Takeaways

1. Embrace a flexible leadership style that encourages team autonomy while providing direction.
2. Foster open communication and encourage regular feedback from team members.
3. Create incentive programs that motivate diverse team members and drive key sales behaviors.
4. Manage performance with continuous feedback and tailored coaching.
5. Empower your team with the tools and opportunities for professional growth.

6. Build a culture of collaboration to leverage collective knowledge and drive innovation.

Food for Thought: Effective sales team management is an art that balances the individual's need for growth and recognition with the team's collective goals. Remember, your leadership and the culture you foster can make or break the team's performance. How are you shaping the environment to bring out the best in your team?

Actionable Strategies for Sales Team Excellence

In a highly competitive marketplace, sales teams need to employ a strategic approach that combines traditional techniques with innovative methods. Here's how some leading sales teams have used actionable strategies to their advantage.

SMART Goals

Setting goals that are Specific, Measurable, Achievable, Relevant, and Time-bound (SMART) ensures that your team knows exactly what is expected, by when, and the goals are realistic enough to be attainable.

- **Strategy Expansion**: Use SMART goals as a framework for all sales objectives. For example, rather than setting a vague goal like "increase sales," a SMART goal would be "increase sales of Product X by 15% in the Northeast region within the next quarter."

- **Case Study**: HubSpot, a leader in inbound marketing and sales, sets SMART goals for its sales team and shares these goals company-wide to ensure transparency and accountability. This has helped them grow their customer base significantly year over year.

Role Specialization

Role specialization allows sales teams to focus on their strengths, whether that's nurturing new leads, closing deals, or managing ongoing client relationships.

- **Strategy Expansion**: Assess your team's talents and align roles to match strengths and preferences. Regularly rotate roles to create a dynamic environment and prevent stagnancy.

- **Case Study**: Salesforce, a global CRM leader, utilizes role specialization to maximize efficiency. They have dedicated teams for different stages of the sales process, ensuring that prospects are guided by experts at each stage.

Data-Driven Decisions

By leveraging customer relationship management (CRM) data, sales teams can make more informed decisions about where to focus their efforts for the best ROI.

- **Strategy Expansion**: Conduct regular data reviews to adjust strategies in real-time. For instance, if the CRM indicates a high conversion rate for a particular demographic, resources can be allocated to target that group more intensively.

- **Case Study**: Netflix uses data analytics not just for content recommendations but also for sales and marketing strategies. They analyze viewing patterns to identify potential markets for expansion and tailor their sales strategies accordingly.

Continuous Training and Development

Investing in ongoing training and development ensures that

your sales team stays on the cutting edge of sales techniques and industry trends.

- **Strategy Expansion**: Create a continuous learning environment by providing access to the latest sales training resources, workshops, and seminars. Encourage knowledge sharing within the team.

- **Case Study**: Zappos is renowned for its customer service. They provide extensive training to their sales team, encouraging them to go above and beyond in customer interactions, which has been pivotal in building a loyal customer base.

Leveraging Technology

Modern sales teams are augmented with a suite of technological tools that streamline processes and provide valuable insights.

- **Strategy Expansion**: Integrate advanced sales automation and intelligence tools that can help your team identify and focus on high-potential leads and trends.

- **Case Study**: Amazon's sales team leverages big data and AI to predict customer needs and personalize sales strategies, significantly increasing their conversion rates.

Collaborative Selling

Encourage a team-based approach to selling, where team members support each other and leverage collective strengths.

- **Strategy Expansion**: Establish a system where salespeople share leads, insights, and strategies to benefit the entire team.

- **Case Study**: Cisco employs a collaborative selling approach where sales, marketing, and technical teams work together closely, allowing them to present unified solutions to clients and capitalize on cross-selling opportunities.

Summary: Key Takeaways

1. Set SMART goals for precise, measurable, and timely objectives.

2. Assign roles that play to each team member's strengths and rotate to foster growth.

3. Make data-driven decisions to fine-tune sales strategies and focus on high-yield activities.

4. Invest in continuous training to ensure the team's skills remain competitive.

5. Utilize technology to enhance sales efforts and customer insights.

6. Foster a collaborative selling environment for shared success and learning.

Food for Thought: As you reflect on these strategies, consider how your team can implement these practices. What existing structures can you leverage, and where might you need to innovate to stay ahead in your industry? Your ability to adapt these strategies to your unique team dynamics will be the ultimate test of your sales leadership.

Food for Thought:

- Reflect on the role of a sales team beyond just revenue generation—think brand ambassadors, customer feedback loops, and market intelligence.

- Contemplate how a diverse team can provide a competitive edge in understanding and reaching different customer segments.

- Consider how the principles of servant leadership can transform your approach to managing a sales team.

Summary: Building and managing a sales team is akin to conducting an orchestra. Each member has a part to play, and when harmonized under skilled leadership, the result can be a symphony that resonates with customers and drives sales. Barbara Corcoran's story exemplifies the power of a visionary leader in assembling a top-performing team. By focusing on the recruitment of complementary talent, fostering continuous improvement, and creating a culture of motivation and reward, you can construct a sales force that not only meets targets but also sets new benchmarks of success.

In conclusion, managing a sales team is not a one-size-fits-all endeavor. It requires a tailored approach that considers the unique dynamics of your team and the goals of your organization. The strategies and anecdotes outlined here provide a blueprint for assembling a powerhouse sales team and leading it to exceed expectations.

Chapter 26:

Scaling Sales Operations

Introduction: Scaling sales operations is the cornerstone of sustainable growth. This chapter is a deep dive into how to grow your sales efforts effectively and efficiently, building upon the foundations you've laid with a single team and expanding that success across the board.

The Foundation – A Tale of Expansion: Let's look at Salesforce, a company that started in a small apartment in San Francisco and grew to a multi-billion-dollar enterprise. Their success hinged on their ability to scale sales operations rapidly while maintaining the quality of customer interaction and service.

Developing a Scalable Sales Model

A scalable sales model is the cornerstone of any business poised for expansion. It allows a company to increase its sales capacity without a corresponding increase in its cost base. Here are the elements of a scalable sales model, illuminated by real-life case studies.

Replicable Success

Creating a sales model that can be replicated is all about consistency and predictability in sales processes.

- **Strategy Expansion**: Standardize your sales approach through training, scripts, and procedures that have been tested and proven. Every new salesperson should be able to follow the model and achieve similar results.

- **Case Study**: Dropbox's referral program is a perfect example of replicable success. They incentivize users to spread the word, effectively turning their customer base into a sales team, and this strategy can be replicated across markets and customer segments.

Structured Systems

Systems should be in place to support sales teams as they ramp up their efforts. This includes everything from customer management to order fulfillment.

- **Strategy Expansion**: Invest in systems that automate and streamline the sales process, such as CRM and sales automation tools, which reduce the manual workload and allow salespeople to focus on closing deals.

- **Case Study**: HubSpot has mastered structured systems with its CRM platform, which allows businesses to scale their sales processes by automating tasks, tracking customer interactions, and managing sales pipelines efficiently.

Growth-Ready Infrastructure

A scalable model necessitates infrastructure that can grow with the business. This means having the right tools, technology, and team structure.

- **Strategy Expansion**: Build an infrastructure that can support a larger volume of sales without bottlenecks. This could mean cloud-based tools that allow for easy expansion or modular team structures that can grow as needed.

- **Case Study**: Shopify provides a scalable platform for merchants, which can support businesses from startup to enterprise level with minimal changes to the underlying sales infrastructure. This has allowed them to grow rapidly and support a large user base without a proportional increase in overhead.

Leveraging Outsourcing and Partnerships

Sometimes, the key to scalability is knowing when to outsource or form partnerships.

- **Strategy Expansion**: Identify non-core activities that can be outsourced and seek strategic partnerships that can extend your sales capabilities without adding fixed costs.

- **Case Study**: Alibaba, the Chinese e-commerce giant, has scaled its sales and distribution model globally by forming partnerships with local businesses and logistics companies, rather than building its own infrastructure from scratch.

Continuous Optimization

A scalable sales model is never static. It requires continuous refinement and optimization based on data and feedback.

- **Strategy Expansion**: Use data analytics to continually refine your sales process. Monitor KPIs and stay flexible, ready to adjust your model based on performance metrics.

- **Case Study**: Netflix constantly optimizes its sales model by using viewership data to not only recommend content but also to decide which shows to produce, thus ensuring they invest in content that has a high likelihood of return.

Summary: Key Takeaways

1. Replicate successful sales practices to ensure consistent performance across the board.

2. Implement structured systems that streamline the sales process and minimize manual work.

3. Build a sales infrastructure that is ready to handle and support growth.

4. Consider outsourcing and partnerships for scalability without heavy investments.

5. Continuously optimize the sales model based on performance data and feedback.

Food for Thought:

Reflect on how these elements can be applied or are already functioning within your sales model. Consider the weakest links in your current model and prioritize strengthening those areas to support future growth. How can you maintain the quality of your sales process as you scale?

Daily Operations – Task and Training

The rhythm of daily operations in sales teams is characterized by dynamic interactions and a relentless push towards targets. Integrating strategic and interpersonal skills in daily tasks and training is essential. Here's how successful sales teams do it, with real-life case studies for context.

Routine Assessments

Ongoing evaluation of sales processes keeps a team agile and effective.

- **Strategy Expansion**: Regularly review sales metrics and KPIs. Use tools like sales analytics software to track performance and identify areas for improvement.
- **Case Study**: Salesforce, a leader in CRM, constantly assesses its sales team's performance using its own analytics and reporting tools. This allows for quick adjustments in strategies, leading to consistent growth in sales efficiency.

Sales Playbook Development

A comprehensive sales playbook ensures all team members are on the same page.

- **Strategy Expansion**: Document successful sales calls, emails, presentations, and close techniques. Update the playbook with new insights and successful tactics.
- **Case Study**: Slack's sales team uses detailed playbooks that guide them through various customer engagement scenarios, ensuring they provide consistent and effective responses that drive sales.

Cross-Training

Cross-training not only creates a more flexible team but also promotes better understanding and collaboration.

- **Strategy Expansion**: Implement training sessions where sales team members learn about different roles and functions, such as marketing strategies or customer success principles.

- **Case Study**: At Google, cross-functional training programs help sales teams understand the broader context of their products and services, leading to more strategic and informed sales conversations.

Daily Stand-ups

Quick daily meetings keep everyone aligned and accountable.

- **Strategy Expansion**: Conduct brief daily stand-up meetings to share successes, challenges, and goals for the day.

- **Case Study**: Atlassian uses daily stand-ups not just for its software development teams but also in sales, keeping the team focused and in sync.

Continuous Learning Programs

In the rapidly changing landscape of sales, continuous learning is key.

- **Strategy Expansion**: Offer ongoing training programs, webinars, and learning sessions to keep the sales team updated on the latest trends, tools, and sales methodologies.

- **Case Study**: HubSpot Academy provides free training and certifications not just to its customers but also to its sales team, ensuring they are well-equipped with the latest inbound sales techniques.

Summary: Key Takeaways

1. Regular assessments can identify and rectify inefficiencies in the sales process.

2. A robust and evolving sales playbook is a vital resource for guiding the sales team's approach.

3. Cross-training enhances team versatility and comprehensive understanding of the business.

4. Daily stand-ups encourage accountability and team cohesion.

5. Continuous learning ensures the sales team evolves with the changing market and technologies.

Food for Thought: What mechanisms do you have in place to ensure that your sales team's daily operations are leading toward the larger strategic goals? How can you foster a culture of continuous improvement and learning?

Anecdote - Efficiency Meets Humanity: A sales director named Maria discovered that her team was spending too much time on administrative tasks. By introducing a CRM tool that automated mundane tasks, her team could focus more on building relationships with clients, ultimately doubling their sales output.

Strategies for Scaling Sales

Scaling sales is an art that combines the use of technology, data analysis, and team structure to expand a business's market presence. This chapter will delve into strategies that successful sales teams employ to grow their operations effectively.

Leveraging Technology

The right technology can be a game-changer for scaling sales.

- **Strategy Expansion**: Implement CRM systems like Salesforce or HubSpot to automate lead tracking, customer communications, and sales pipeline management. Additionally, tools like Outreach or Salesloft can automate and personalize customer outreach.

- **Case Study**: Zoom Video Communications effectively used Salesforce's CRM to manage a surge in leads and customers during the rapid shift to remote work. The technology allowed them to scale their sales process to meet the increased demand efficiently.

Data Analysis

Making sense of data is crucial to inform scaling strategies.

- **Strategy Expansion**: Utilize data analytics to gain insights into sales performance, customer behavior, and market trends. Use tools like Tableau or Microsoft Power BI for visual analytics and reporting.

- **Case Study**: Netflix uses big data analytics to not only recommend content to users but also to decide which new shows to produce. Similarly, in sales, data analysis can predict which products will be successful and which markets to target.

Specialization and Segmentation

Focused roles can drive efficiency and effectiveness in the sales process.

- **Strategy Expansion**: Designate specialized roles such as lead qualifiers, inside sales reps, account executives, and customer success managers to streamline the sales process. Use market segmentation to tailor sales strategies to different customer groups.

- **Case Study**: Oracle has segmented its sales force by industry, solution type, and customer size, allowing sales reps to become experts in their specific domain and more effectively sell to their target segments.

Sales Enablement

Empower your sales team with the right content, tools, and training.

- **Strategy Expansion**: Develop a sales enablement strategy that provides sales teams with the resources they need to sell more effectively. This includes on-demand access to content like case studies, product sheets, and competitive intelligence.

- **Case Study**: LinkedIn's sales enablement strategy includes a comprehensive training program and a rich repository of sales materials, enabling their teams to scale their efforts across various markets and industries.

Iterative Process Improvements

Continually refine your sales process based on feedback and results.

- **Strategy Expansion**: Adopt a culture of continuous improvement where sales processes are regularly reviewed and optimized based on quantitative and qualitative feedback.

- **Case Study**: Toyota's philosophy of 'Kaizen', or continuous improvement, has been adopted by sales organizations like Zappos. They consistently refine their sales approaches based on customer feedback and operational data, allowing for sustainable growth.

Summary: Key Takeaways

1. Technology is an enabler of scale; invest in CRM and automation to handle increased volumes.
2. Data analytics provide the insights needed to make smart scaling decisions.
3. Role specialization within the sales team ensures that expertise is developed and utilized effectively.
4. Sales enablement equips the team with the necessary tools and information to succeed at scale.
5. Iterative improvements ensure that processes evolve and adapt to changing needs.

Food for Thought: As your sales operations grow, how can you maintain the quality of your sales interactions? What role does technology play in your strategy to scale, and how can you ensure your team is making the most of the data at their disposal?

Actionable Strategies for a Winning Sales Team

Building a winning sales team is not just about hiring the right people; it's also about nurturing and developing their talents as the business grows. Here's how some of the most successful sales organizations have done it:

Hire for Growth

You want team members who can not only sell but also evolve with the company.

- **Strategy Expansion**: In addition to the necessary sales skills, evaluate potential hires for leadership qualities and the ability to take on more complex sales strategies or management roles.

- **Case Study**: Google is known for its rigorous hiring process, focusing not just on the candidate's current capabilities but also on their potential for growth. They often pose hypothetical problems that test a candidate's ability to learn and adapt, crucial for scaling operations.

Focus on Training

A systematic training program is key to consistency and quality in scaling sales.

- **Strategy Expansion**: Your training program should cover product knowledge, sales skills, and company culture. It should be adaptable and regularly updated to reflect market changes and new sales strategies.

- **Case Study**: IBM has a world-renowned sales training program, IBM Global Sales School, that equips sales professionals with the skills needed to adapt to various customer needs and selling situations, which has been integral to their sustained growth.

Continuous Improvement

A learning environment is vital for sales teams to adapt and thrive.

- **Strategy Expansion**: Build a continuous learning culture that values upskilling and reskilling. Use performance metrics not just for evaluations but also to guide development plans.

- **Case Study**: At Amazon, the principle of "Day 1" culture fosters continuous learning and agility among its teams. This mindset encourages sales teams to innovate, experiment, and constantly seek improvements, which is key for scaling in dynamic markets.

Summary: Key Takeaways

1. Hiring for growth means looking beyond current needs to the future potential of candidates.

2. Training is not a one-time event but a continuous process that scales with your team.

3. Embracing continuous improvement ensures that your sales strategy stays relevant and effective.

Food for Thought: Reflect on how you can structure your hiring processes to identify individuals who will grow with your company. Consider the role that ongoing training plays in your sales team's success and how a culture of improvement can be embedded within your team.

Food for Thought:

- How can the concept of 'sales velocity' — the speed at which leads move through your pipeline and turn into revenue — be increased sustainably?

- Reflect on how a strong company culture can influence the scalability of sales operations.

- Consider the balance between sales automation and personal touch — how can technology empower personal connection rather than replace it?

Summary: Scaling sales operations isn't just about growing numbers; it's about smart growth — increasing efficiency, maintaining or improving quality, and ensuring that the customer experience scales too. Salesforce's expansion from a modest startup to a global leader in CRM software is a testament to a well-executed scaling strategy. By adopting the right technologies, focusing on data-driven strategies, and investing in people, any sales organization can set itself up for scalable success.

Maria's anecdote is a practical example of how focusing on efficiency and relationship-building can lead to significant improvements in sales output. Sales operations can scale effectively when they are systemized, when there's continuous training and development, and when technology is leveraged to enhance, not replace, the human element of sales.

In closing, the ability to scale sales operations effectively is what can turn a promising business into a market leader. The insights and case studies shared in this chapter serve as a blueprint for sales leaders aiming to expand their influence and reach without losing the essence of what made their sales efforts successful in the first place.

Chapter 27:

The Ethics of Selling

Introduction: Ethics in selling is not just a moral compass; it's the very foundation that can make or break the trust between a salesperson and a client. This chapter will uncover the indispensable role of ethics in sales, which is crucial for long-term success.

The Importance of Ethics – A Story of Trust: Consider the rise and fall of Elizabeth Holmes and her company, Theranos. Once celebrated as a revolutionary in the health technology space, her downfall was rooted in unethical sales and business practices, leading to massive financial and reputational damage. This cautionary tale underscores the significance of ethics in business.

Building an Ethical Sales Framework:

- **Transparency**: Ensure that honesty is at the core of all sales communications.

- **Integrity**: Uphold moral principles by delivering on promises and acknowledging mistakes.
- **Respect**: Treat every client with dignity and respect, regardless of the potential sale value.

Daily Operations – Task and Training:

1. **Ethical Decision-Making Training**: Incorporate ethical scenarios in sales training programs.
2. **Role-Playing**: Engage in role-playing exercises to navigate ethical dilemmas.
3. **Regular Ethics Audits**: Conduct periodic reviews to ensure sales practices are ethical.

Anecdote - The Honorable Sale: Dan, a pharmaceutical sales rep, was faced with pushing a new drug that he knew wasn't the best option for some patients. He chose to discuss alternative treatments with doctors, earning their trust and building a reputation for integrity, which eventually led to an increase in sales across the board.

Strategies for Ethical Selling:

- **Customer-Centric Selling**: Prioritize the customer's needs and the value they gain from your product.
- **Authenticity**: Be genuine in interactions; customers can sense when a salesperson is being disingenuous.
- **Accountability**: Take responsibility for the product and its outcomes.

Actionable Strategies:

1. **Create an Ethics Charter**: Draft a document that outlines the ethical standards and expectations for your sales team.

2. **Transparent Reporting**: Establish a transparent reporting system for both successes and failures.

3. **Ethical Incentives**: Design incentive programs that reward ethical behavior as well as sales targets.

Food for Thought:

- Consider how an ethical breach can have long-term consequences for personal and company reputations.

- Reflect on the role of ethics in customer retention and lifetime value.

- Debate the notion that in sales, the ends justify the means, especially in highly competitive markets.

Summary: In a world where consumers are increasingly aware and concerned about ethical practices, the salesperson's role is more than just selling; it's about fostering trust and demonstrating integrity. The story of Elizabeth Holmes serves as a powerful reminder that unethical practices, even if initially successful, can lead to disastrous outcomes. Conversely, Dan's example illustrates that ethical behavior can differentiate a salesperson and lead to sustainable success.

This chapter implores sales professionals to consider the ethical implications of their actions. By establishing a framework that promotes transparency, integrity, and respect, sales teams can create lasting relationships with customers that are based on trust.

In closing, integrating ethics into the sales process is a strategic move that not only protects the company's reputation but also contributes to a positive brand image and customer loyalty. The real-life case studies and strategies discussed in this chapter provide a blueprint for maintaining high ethical standards in sales practices.

Chapter 28:

*Continuous Learning
and Adaptation*

Introduction The landscape of sales is constantly evolving. With the advent of new technologies, shifts in consumer behavior, and the fluctuating economy, the ability to adapt and continuously learn is not just advantageous – it's essential. This chapter will delve into the essence of staying agile and educated in the world of sales.

Case Study: The Tech Titans Consider the tech industry, where giants like Google and Apple reside. Their sales strategies adapt swiftly to market changes and technological advancements. They foster environments of continuous learning, where sales teams are up-to-date with the latest trends, tools, and methodologies. These organizations demonstrate that a learning culture is integral to sales success.

The Learning Salesperson's Mindset

The mindset of a salesperson can be the differentiator between good and great. Sales professionals who embody curiosity, flexibility, and a growth orientation not only hit their targets more consistently but also contribute to a culture that fosters long-term success.

Curiosity

Curiosity drives salespeople to delve deeper into the 'whys' behind customer behavior and the 'hows' of product development, giving them an edge in understanding and meeting customer needs.

- **Strategy Expansion**: Encourage sales teams to ask open-ended questions and genuinely listen to customers' responses. This practice can reveal underlying customer motivations and create opportunities for more tailored pitches.
- **Real-Life Example**: A representative from HubSpot once shared how their curiosity about a client's hesitancy led to a discovery of a feature mismatch. By understanding the specific needs, they were able to suggest an alternative HubSpot service that better met the client's needs, securing a long-term partnership.

Flexibility

The best sales strategies are often responsive rather than rigid, allowing salespeople to navigate the complex and dynamic waters of customer relations and market trends.

- **Strategy Expansion**: Create scenarios during training that require quick thinking and strategy shifts to build this skill.
- **Case Study**: Zappos is celebrated for its customer service flexibility. Sales staff are encouraged to go off-

script and use their judgment to satisfy customers, resulting in impressive customer loyalty and high sales conversion rates.

Growth Orientation

Top sales performers view each day as an opportunity to learn something new, never settling into complacency.

- **Strategy Expansion**: Implement mentorship programs where less experienced salespeople can learn from seasoned veterans, fostering a culture of continuous learning and improvement.

- **Case Study**: At Salesforce, continuous learning is part of the company's ethos. Their online learning platform, Trailhead, is not just for customers but also for employees, encouraging them to constantly develop new skills and stay at the forefront of the CRM industry.

Summary: Key Takeaways

1. Curiosity leads to deeper customer insights and better solution matching.
2. Flexibility allows salespeople to adapt to customer needs and changing market conditions.
3. Growth orientation ensures that sales skills and product knowledge continuously evolve.

Food for Thought: Reflect on how a learning mindset can transform challenges into learning opportunities. Consider how you can foster a culture that values curiosity, flexibility, and growth.

The examples and strategies in this chapter should illustrate how the mindset of each salesperson contributes to the collective success of the sales team. By maintaining a focus on learning, sales teams can adapt to industry changes, innovate in their approach, and consistently deliver value to customers, thereby driving sales success.

Daily Learning Tasks and Training Programs:

1. **Market Analysis Exercises**: Stay abreast of market trends and how they affect sales strategies.

2. **Product Knowledge Sessions**: Regularly update the team on product enhancements and new offerings.

3. **Soft Skills Development**: Conduct workshops on communication, negotiation, and emotional intelligence.

Real-Life Anecdote: The Adaptive Sales Leader Sara Blakely, founder of Spanx, sold fax machines door-to-door before becoming a self-made billionaire. Her story is one of adaptation and persistence, where continuous learning from each rejection led her to develop Spanx and revolutionize the women's undergarment industry.

Detailed Strategies for Learning and Adapting

In a competitive sales landscape, the ability to learn from various data points and adapt accordingly is critical. This chapter outlines the strategic utilization of sales data, customer feedback, and competitor analysis to inform and refine sales tactics.

Leverage Sales Data

Data is the compass that guides a sales team's strategic direction.

Harnessing it effectively can unveil patterns and opportunities otherwise overlooked.

- **Strategy Expansion**: Train your team to interpret sales data not just in terms of numbers but as a narrative that tells what works, what doesn't, and why.

- **Real-Life Example**: Netflix's algorithm is a prime example of leveraging user data to drive sales and retention by recommending shows and movies that keep subscribers engaged.

Customer Feedback Loops

A robust feedback loop is a treasure trove of insights directly from the market, providing real-world validation or criticism.

- **Strategy Expansion**: Use automated survey tools post-sale to gather feedback and make it a routine for sales reps to follow-up for detailed reviews on the customer experience.

- **Case Study**: Slack's platform continuously evolves based on user feedback, which has been instrumental in its growth, showing how customer insights can lead to successful product adaptations.

Competitor Analysis

Understanding your competition is about carving a niche for your brand that is defined by its unique value proposition.

- **Strategy Expansion**: Conduct SWOT (Strengths, Weaknesses, Opportunities, Threats) analyses not only of your own company but also of competitors to gain a multi-dimensional view of the market.

- **Case Study**: Samsung's rise in the smartphone

market was propelled by its meticulous analysis of competitors, which it then used to innovate features that were absent in the market, catering to unmet customer needs.

Summary: Key Takeaways

1. Sales data can provide a narrative that helps refine sales strategies.

2. Customer feedback is essential for continuous product and service improvement.

3. Competitor analysis should be used for differentiation and innovation, not imitation.

Food for Thought: Think about how the integration of these detailed strategies can create a feedback-rich environment conducive to learning and adapting. What systems and routines can be established to make learning and adapting a seamless part of the sales process?

This chapter should serve to underscore the importance of a strategic approach to learning and adapting within the sales framework. By continuously analyzing data, listening to customers, and observing competitors, sales teams can remain agile and innovative, securing their place at the forefront of their respective industries.

Actionable Adaptation Strategies

Adaptation in the sales industry isn't just about reacting to changes; it's about proactively preparing for them. This chapter delves into the implementation of peer learning, adaptation workshops, and mentorship as strategies for building a resilient and adaptable sales team.

Peer Learning Sessions

Promoting an environment where sales professionals can exchange knowledge enhances the collective skill set of the team.

- **Strategy Expansion**: Designate regular "Sales Sharing" meetings where team members present a successful sale case or a challenging situation and the lessons learned.
- **Real-Life Example**: Google is known for its TGIF meetings where employees share successes and failures, encouraging a culture of transparency and learning.

Adaptation Workshops

Simulating sales scenarios in a controlled environment allows salespeople to practice and hone their adaptability.

- **Strategy Expansion**: Create monthly themed workshops focusing on different aspects of the sales cycle, like prospecting or closing, with actors to provide a realistic interaction experience.
- **Case Study**: Atlassian runs quarterly "ShipIt Days" where teams have 24 hours to work on projects outside of their regular responsibilities, fostering innovation and adaptability.

Mentorship Programs

Matching less experienced salespeople with mentors can accelerate their development and enhance their ability to adapt.

- **Strategy Expansion**: Develop a structured mentorship

path with clear objectives, regular check-ins, and a feedback loop for both mentors and mentees.

- **Case Study**: General Electric's renowned reverse mentoring program, which pairs younger employees with executive team members, demonstrates the mutual benefits of mentorship in adapting to new trends and technologies.

Summary: Key Takeaways

1. Peer learning can democratize knowledge and empower sales teams.

2. Adaptation workshops provide safe spaces to practice and refine sales techniques.

3. Mentorship programs accelerate learning and adaptation for sales professionals.

Food for Thought: Consider how these strategies might be integrated into your existing sales training programs. How can you measure the impact of these adaptation strategies on your team's performance?

Incorporating these actionable adaptation strategies will help in creating a proactive sales team capable of navigating the evolving landscape of sales with agility and confidence. By learning from each other, practicing for various scenarios, and embracing mentorship, a sales team can significantly improve its effectiveness and adaptability.

Food for Thought:

- Reflect on how resistance to change might be the biggest barrier to sales success.

- How does one measure the effectiveness of continuous learning and adaptation in a sales role?
- Debate the statement: "In sales, if you're not moving forward, you're falling behind."

Summary: This chapter implores sales professionals to embed continuous learning and adaptation into their daily routines. The success stories of tech titans and entrepreneurs like Sara Blakely emphasize that learning is a journey without a final destination. It's the ongoing process of acquiring new knowledge, skills, and experiences that empowers sales professionals to thrive in dynamic environments.

Adopting a learner's mindset and implementing a structured approach to education and adaptation can transform a sales team's capabilities and results. The detailed strategies and actionable steps provided in this chapter serve as a blueprint for sales professionals committed to excellence through perpetual growth.

To encapsulate the concept, consider incorporating case studies from companies like HubSpot, which has built an academy for its sales teams and clients, highlighting the significance of continuous education. Or take the example of Amazon, where customer feedback is integral to their sales strategy, showcasing the power of adaptation. By examining these companies, readers will grasp how continuous learning and adaptation are not just theoretical concepts but practical tools wielded by the most successful sales teams worldwide.

In conclusion, the path of continuous learning and adaptation in sales is marked by an unwavering commitment to self-improvement, resilience in the face of change, and a proactive approach to evolving market dynamics. This chapter is an essential read for those who aspire to not only keep up with the pace of change but to lead the charge in their respective industries.

Chapter 29:

Leveraging Feedback and Criticism

Introduction In the cutthroat world of sales, feedback and criticism are as inevitable as they are valuable. The most successful sales professionals don't just tolerate feedback; they actively seek it and use it to their advantage. This chapter delves into strategies to leverage feedback and criticism to sharpen your sales approach, boost your performance, and elevate your customer relationships.

Real-Life Anecdote: The Humble Titan Take, for example, the legendary Jack Welch, former CEO of General Electric. He was known for his candid management style and commitment to constant improvement, often soliciting frank, unvarnished feedback from his employees. Welch's leadership transformed GE, showing how powerful feedback can be when it's taken seriously and acted upon.

Detailed Explanations:

1. **Types of Feedback**:
   - *Constructive*: Offers insights and suggestions for improvement.
   - *Evaluative*: Provides an assessment of performance against set standards.
   - *Appreciative*: Recognizes strengths and achievements.

2. **Receiving Criticism**:
   - *Listen Actively*: Don't just hear; listen and understand the feedback.
   - *Stay Calm*: Maintain composure to process the feedback effectively.
   - *Clarify and Reflect*: Ensure you fully comprehend the feedback before responding.

Daily Tasks and Training Program:

1. **Daily Reflection Journal**: Record and reflect on the feedback received each day.

2. **Weekly Review Meetings**: Discuss feedback with mentors or managers to create an action plan.

3. **Role-Playing Scenarios**: Practice responding to criticism constructively.

Case Study: The Responsive Retailers Zappos, the online shoe and clothing retailer, is renowned for its customer service. They not only welcome customer feedback but also act on it swiftly, transforming potentially negative experiences into loyalty-building opportunities. Zappos' model shows how feedback can be an engine for growth and customer satisfaction.

Actionable Strategies:

- **Feedback Systems**: Implement systems to collect

regular feedback from customers and team members.

- **Criticism Training Sessions**: Train sales teams on how to receive and process criticism effectively.

- **Feedback Loop Meetings**: Regularly scheduled meetings to discuss feedback and create improvement plans.

Food for Thought:

- How does one distinguish between useful criticism and noise?

- In what ways can negative feedback be more valuable than positive feedback?

- What methods can be used to encourage customers to provide honest feedback?

Summary: Embracing feedback and criticism is not a sign of weakness but a strategy for excellence. Jack Welch's legacy and Zappos' success story underscore the transformative power of a feedback-centric approach. This chapter has outlined the various types of feedback, the psychological strategies for receiving criticism, and the practical steps to integrate feedback into the daily sales process.

Feedback is a gift that, when unwrapped with skill and care, can lead to unprecedented sales success. It is a catalyst for personal development and a compass that guides sales professionals toward better practices, stronger relationships, and ultimately, more sales. This chapter is not just a roadmap for managing feedback but an invitation to view feedback as the cornerstone of a successful and dynamic sales career.

Chapter 30:

Networking and Building
Industry Relationships

Introduction

The art of selling extends far beyond the ability to pitch a product or close a deal. It is, at its core, about building relationships. In sales, your network is your net worth, and successful networking can transform your career. This chapter will take you on a journey through the art of networking, illustrating its importance with real-life case studies and providing you with the tools to build a robust web of industry connections.

Real-Life Anecdote: The Connector

Consider the story of Keith Ferrazzi, the author of "Never Eat Alone" and a master networker. Ferrazzi climbed the ladder from a working-class background to the heights of professional success by masterfully leveraging the power of relationships, transforming acquaintances into allies throughout his career.

Detailed Explanations:

- **Importance of Networking**: In-depth exploration of how networking can lead to new opportunities, insights, and increased sales.

- **Building Trust**: Strategies for establishing trust and credibility within your network.

- **Networking Channels**: Guidance on using various channels such as industry conferences, online platforms, and direct outreach to build your network.

Case Study: The Synergistic Software Sellers

Salesforce, a leader in CRM software, has an enviable network of industry partnerships. By creating a vast ecosystem of customers, developers, and service providers, Salesforce has turned networking into a strategic asset, driving growth and innovation.

Daily Tasks and Training Program:

1. **Daily Relationship Goals**: Set a goal to reach out to a specific number of new or existing contacts daily.

2. **Industry Event Attendance**: Schedule and attend at least two industry-related events each month.

3. **Networking Skills Workshops**: Regular training sessions focused on refining interpersonal skills and effective communication.

Actionable Strategies:

- **CRM for Networking**: Use a CRM system to keep track of your contacts, their interests, and follow-up schedules.

- **Elevator Pitch**: Develop and practice a compelling personal pitch for spontaneous networking opportunities.

- **Mentorship Program**: Create or join a program to connect with more experienced professionals in your industry.

Food for Thought:

- Reflect on the role of authenticity in networking. How can you remain genuine while also aiming to sell?

- Consider the balance between online and in-person networking in the digital age. What unique advantages does each offer?

- Think about the concept of 'giving before you get'. How can helping others advance your networking goals?

Summary:

Networking is not just about collecting contacts; it's about planting the seeds of mutual benefit that blossom into career-long relationships. Keith Ferrazzi's ascent and Salesforce's ecosystem exemplify how nurturing these connections can create a competitive edge. Through strategic outreach, trust-building, and a commitment to continuous relationship management, any sales professional can grow a powerful network.

This chapter has provided a playbook for creating a rich tapestry of industry connections, ensuring that whether you're reaching out via LinkedIn, shaking hands at a conference, or sharing expertise in a workshop, you are consistently adding value and weaving stronger threads into your career network.

Remember, the most effective sales network is one that is both wide, reaching across industries and roles, and deep, marked by genuine, trusted relationships. As we've seen through various case studies, the benefits of such a network are boundless. Your task now is to take these strategies and insights, apply them with care and attention, and construct your own network—one connection at a time.

Chapter 31:

Personal Branding for Sales Professionals

Introduction

The sales landscape is fiercely competitive. To distinguish oneself, it's not enough to be a great salesperson; you need to be a memorable one. Personal branding is the key to standing out. It's the sum total of impressions you leave on your clients and colleagues – a unique blend of skills, experiences, and personal flair that makes you, you. Let's explore the strategies behind successful personal brands and how to cultivate your own.

The Tale of the Memorable Maven

Consider the legend of Zig Ziglar, a salesman who became a world-renowned motivational speaker and trainer. Ziglar didn't just sell cookware; he sold a philosophy of positive thinking and goal-setting. His personal brand was built on the foundation of his infectious enthusiasm and unwavering belief in the potential of others.

The Power of a Personal Brand

- **Recognition**: A well-crafted personal brand makes you easily identifiable in the industry.

- **Trust**: When people know who you are and what you stand for, they're more likely to trust you.

- **Career Trajectory**: A strong brand can lead to better job opportunities, speaking engagements, and more.

Case Study: The Charismatic Consultant

Deloitte's personal branding initiative for their consultants demonstrates how a company encourages employees to create personal brands aligned with corporate values. This synergy increases both individual and corporate visibility, creating a network of ambassadors in the market.

Daily Tasks and Training Program:

1. **Reflective Journaling**: Identify your strengths, values, and passions through daily writing exercises.

2. **Social Media Presence**: Dedicate time each day to post thought leadership content or industry commentary on professional networks like LinkedIn.

3. **Speaking Engagements**: Aim to participate in or lead workshops and seminars to enhance your public speaking skills and visibility.

Actionable Strategies:

- **Unique Value Proposition (UVP)**: Develop and hone a statement that encapsulates what you offer that no one else does.

- **Consistent Messaging**: Ensure your communication across all platforms reflects your UVP and brand voice.
- **Professional Imagery**: Invest in professional headshots and maintain a consistent visual theme on your social profiles.

Food for Thought:

- How does your personal brand reflect your professional values?
- What aspects of your personality or expertise are most engaging to your clients or audience?
- In what ways can you leverage your personal brand to create more meaningful interactions with your clients?

Summary:

Your personal brand is your reputation, and in sales, your reputation is your most valuable asset. Like Zig Ziglar, who sold not just products but a promise of personal growth, your brand should tell a story about who you are and the value you bring. The case of Deloitte's branding initiative exemplifies that personal branding doesn't just elevate the individual – it lifts the entire organization.

In cultivating your brand, remember to be authentic, consistent, and visible. Use daily tasks like reflective journaling and social media engagement to continually refine and express your brand. Attend speaking engagements to build your reputation as an expert and thought leader.

From the actionable strategies discussed, your mission is to create a personal brand that resonates with your network and sets you apart from the crowd. By doing so, you not only advance your career but also become a beacon in your industry, guiding others and illuminating opportunities. Embrace this journey of personal branding, and watch as doors open to a future of boundless potential.

Chapter 32:

Innovation in Sales Techniques

Introduction

In the realm of sales, innovation isn't just about having a cutting-edge product; it's about pioneering new ways to connect, convince, and close. This chapter dives into how innovative sales techniques can revolutionize your approach and outcomes, providing a deeper understanding of the strategic and interpersonal skills required to excel in today's market.

Innovate Like Edison

Thomas Edison, known for his prolific inventions, was also a master salesman. He didn't just create the light bulb; he sold the concept of electric light to a world accustomed to gas lamps and candles. Edison understood that innovation in sales was as critical as the innovation of the product.

The New Sales Formula

- **Customization Over Standardization**: Tailoring your approach to individual customer needs instead of one-size-fits-all.

- **Education as a Tool**: Providing value through education positions you as a trusted advisor, not just a vendor.

- **Technology Integration**: Using CRMs, AI, and data analytics to inform and streamline the sales process.

Real-Life Case Study: The Tech Titans

Salesforce, a global leader in CRM, epitomizes innovation in sales through technology. Their use of cloud computing revolutionized how sales teams interact with data, leading to more personalized and effective sales strategies.

Daily Tasks and Training Program:

1. **Market Research**: Allocate time daily to study market trends and emerging technologies in sales.

2. **Role-playing Scenarios**: Regularly practice new sales techniques with team members to refine your approach.

3. **Technology Proficiency**: Dedicate time each week to learn about new sales tools and platforms.

Actionable Strategies:

- **Adaptability**: Stay flexible and be ready to pivot your sales strategy based on real-time feedback and market conditions.

- **Collaborative Selling**: Engage with different

departments to provide comprehensive solutions that meet all facets of customer needs.

- **Social Selling**: Utilize social media to understand customer challenges and engage in meaningful conversations.

Food for Thought:

- Consider how your sales techniques can evolve with changing consumer behaviors.

- Reflect on the tools and platforms that can enhance your sales approach. Are you making the most of them?

- How can you cultivate a culture of continuous learning and innovation within your sales team?

Summary:

Innovation in sales isn't just a buzzword; it's a strategic necessity. Thomas Edison taught us that selling the concept is as crucial as the invention itself. Adopting innovative sales techniques means stepping out of the traditional playbook and embracing a customized, educational, and technology-driven approach.

Salesforce's example shows us that the right tools can lead to a paradigm shift in how sales are conducted and managed. By integrating new technology into daily practices, training rigorously on emerging techniques, and fostering adaptability, sales professionals can remain at the forefront of their industry.

As a sales professional, your ability to innovate is critical. Whether it's through leveraging technology like CRM systems, adopting social selling practices, or finding novel ways to educate and engage with customers, the innovation in your sales techniques can be the differentiator that sets you apart.

In conclusion, the world of sales is continuously evolving. By staying abreast of new technologies, refining your approach, and fostering an innovative mindset, you can not only meet but exceed the expectations of the modern consumer. Let the case studies and strategies outlined in this chapter be your guide to a future where your sales process isn't just effective, it's revolutionary.

Chapter 33:

Conquering Sales Slumps

Introduction

Every sales professional will face a slump at some point in their career. This chapter isn't just about recognizing the signs of a sales slump but about deploying strategies to overcome it, with insights from successful sales teams and the individual tenacity of famous figures.

Embracing the Slump: The Michael Jordan Philosophy

Even Michael Jordan, one of the greatest basketball players of all time, faced slumps in his career. Yet, he saw these periods not as failures but as opportunities to learn and grow. Jordan's resilience is a testament to conquering personal and professional setbacks, something every sales professional can learn from.

The Anatomy of a Sales Slump

- **Recognition**: Identifying the signs of a slump early.
- **Assessment**: Analyzing the root causes.
- **Action**: Taking steps to counteract the downturn.

Real-Life Case Study: The Turnaround Team

Xerox, once facing a massive decline in sales, turned their fate around by restructuring their sales approach, focusing on solution-based selling, and improving customer relationships. Their comeback story is a masterclass in confronting and overcoming sales adversity.

Daily Tasks and Training Program:

1. **Personal Assessment**: Start each day by evaluating your current sales methods and mindset.
2. **Customer Feedback**: Make it a daily habit to gather and analyze customer feedback.
3. **Skill Enhancement**: Dedicate time each week to develop new sales skills or refine existing ones.

Actionable Strategies:

- **Back to Basics**: Revisit the core principles of sales that may have been overlooked.
- **Realign Goals**: Set new, achievable targets to regain confidence and momentum.
- **Customer Re-engagement**: Reach out to previous customers to re-establish relationships and gather insights.

Food for Thought:

- How can you turn a period of low performance into a learning opportunity?

- Reflect on the triggers that may have led to the slump. How can you mitigate these factors in the future?

- Consider what strategies you can adopt to inject new life into your sales routine.

Summary:

Conquering a sales slump requires a Michael Jordan-like mindset: recognizing setbacks as a springboard for growth. Xerox's story illustrates that even when the odds are stacked against you, a strategic reassessment and proactive engagement can bring about a triumphant turnaround.

The daily tasks and training programs outlined in this chapter encourage constant self-evaluation and customer interaction as a means to stay ahead of potential slumps. By integrating actionable strategies such as getting back to sales fundamentals, realigning goals, and re-engaging with customers, you can navigate through and emerge victorious from sales slumps.

Through real-life anecdotes and case studies, we understand that slumps are part of the sales landscape. Yet, with the right approach—embracing innovation, continuous learning, and customer-centric selling—we can not only conquer these slumps but also use them to propel us to greater heights.

In closing, remember that a sales slump is not the end of your story. It can be the beginning of a new chapter, one where you emerge wiser, more skilled, and more determined. Let the strategies in this chapter be your guide to transforming a period of stagnation into a period of unprecedented growth and success.

Chapter 34:

The Role of Emotion in Selling

Introduction

Sales is not just a transaction; it's a transfer of emotion. The most successful sales professionals understand that emotions drive behavior and that creating an emotional connection can be the key to closing deals. This chapter explores the nuanced role of emotion in selling, with strategies that bring heart to the art of persuasion.

The Science of Emotion in Sales

Recent studies in neuroeconomics show that emotions are integral to decision-making processes. Emotions can disrupt logical thinking paths and pave the way for more intuitive choices - a fact that can significantly impact sales strategies.

Real-Life Case Study: The Empathetic Approach of Apple

Apple Inc. is renowned for its ability to connect with customers on an emotional level. The tech giant doesn't just sell products;

it sells experiences and lifestyles. Their "Think Different" campaign tapped into a collective desire for innovation and individualism, showcasing how empathy can drive brand loyalty and sales.

Daily Tasks and Training Program:

1. **Emotional Intelligence Enhancement**: Practice identifying and managing your emotions and the emotions of others.

2. **Empathy Exercises**: Role-play customer interactions to better understand their needs and concerns.

3. **Storytelling Practice**: Develop compelling stories that connect your product to the customer's emotional desires.

Actionable Strategies:

- **Emotional Mirroring**: Adapt your tone and body language to match your client's, building rapport.

- **Benefit Emotionalization**: Focus on how your product can make the customer feel, not just what it does.

- **Objection Handling with Compassion**: Listen actively to concerns and address them with understanding and care.

Food for Thought:

- Reflect on a recent purchase you made primarily because of how the product made you feel. Can you apply this insight to your selling technique?

- Consider how you can use emotional intelligence to better respond to and connect with clients.

- Think about the last time a customer was upset. How could an empathetic response have changed the outcome?

The Empathy Factor: The Story of a Sales Legend

Zig Ziglar, one of the most celebrated sales trainers, often said, "People don't care how much you know until they know how much you care." His approach to selling was deeply rooted in empathy, which fostered trust and connection, driving countless successful sales.

The Emotional Journey Map

Understanding the customer's emotional journey through the buying process can be transformative. Creating a journey map involves:

- **Awareness**: Acknowledging the customer's initial emotional state.
- **Consideration**: Understanding the emotional factors influencing their consideration of the product.
- **Decision**: Recognizing the emotions at play during the decision-making phase.

Summary:

The integration of emotion into sales isn't a gimmick; it's a critical component of modern selling techniques. From Apple's empathetic brand positioning to Zig Ziglar's advocacy for care in sales interactions, harnessing emotion can turn prospects into passionate customers. The daily tasks and strategies discussed in this chapter provide a roadmap for sales professionals to enhance their emotional intelligence and leverage it for sales success.

Through storytelling, emotional mirroring, and empathetic engagement, sales professionals can create deeper connections with customers. The exercises and anecdotes featured in this chapter serve as a guide to understanding and utilizing emotions in selling, turning transactions into transformative experiences that benefit both the seller and the customer.

In closing, remember that at the heart of every sale is a human being driven by emotions. The ability to engage with those emotions authentically and compassionately is what can set you apart in the crowded marketplace. Let the power of emotion drive your sales to new heights, and watch as your connections with customers deepen and your success in sales multiplies.

Chapter 35:

Cross-Cultural and Global Selling

Introduction

In the tapestry of modern commerce, the threads of cross-cultural interactions are interwoven tighter than ever before. As borders dissolve in the digital age, the ability to sell across cultures is not just an advantage; it's a necessity. This chapter delves into the strategies that equip sales professionals to navigate the richly diverse global marketplace.

The Art of Cross-Cultural Communication

The first step in cross-cultural selling is understanding that communication is more than language. It's about understanding context, non-verbal cues, and cultural nuances. A mastery of cross-cultural communication enables sales professionals to connect with clients from various backgrounds effectively.

Real-Life Case Study: The Global Strategy of Starbucks

Starbucks' expansion into China showcases a masterclass in cross-cultural selling. Rather than imposing its American coffee culture, Starbucks introduced tea-based beverages and localized store designs, respecting China's tea tradition and winning the hearts of the local populace.

Daily Tasks and Training Program:

1. **Cultural Research**: Dedicate time each day to learn about a new culture, focusing on business etiquette and social norms.

2. **Language Learning**: Engage in daily language practice, even if it's just learning key phrases.

3. **Cultural Sensitivity Training**: Regularly participate in workshops to enhance cultural understanding and sensitivity.

Actionable Strategies:

- **Cultural Adaptation**: Tailor your sales approach to align with the cultural expectations and preferences of each market.

- **Active Listening**: Focus on understanding the client's perspective, which can vary significantly across cultures.

- **Local Market Insights**: Utilize local partners or team members' insights to refine your sales strategy.

Food for Thought:

- How do your own cultural biases influence your selling strategy, and how can you address them?

- In what ways can you incorporate respect for a prospect's culture into your sales process?
- Reflect on a time when a lack of cultural understanding impacted a business interaction. What could have been done differently?

The Power of Cultural Intelligence: The Story of Pepsico's Indra Nooyi

Under Indra Nooyi's leadership, Pepsico thrived by embracing cultural intelligence. Nooyi, who grew up in India, leveraged her cross-cultural expertise to tailor products and marketing strategies to diverse global markets, vastly expanding Pepsico's reach.

Building a Cross-Cultural Sales Framework

Successful global selling requires a framework built on:

- **Research**: In-depth understanding of cultural practices and consumer behaviors.
- **Respect**: Genuine respect for different traditions and social mores.
- **Adaptability**: Flexibility in sales approaches to accommodate various cultural expectations.

Summary:

Cross-cultural and global selling is a complex, yet rewarding endeavor that requires an open mind, adaptability, and respect for diversity. By studying cases like Starbucks' cultural sensitivity in China and Indra Nooyi's leadership at Pepsico, sales professionals can appreciate the nuances of selling to a global audience.

This chapter has outlined daily tasks such as cultural research and language learning that can build one's competence in cross-cultural selling. Through actionable strategies like cultural adaptation and leveraging local insights, sales professionals can craft pitches that resonate across cultural divides.

The key takeaway is that in the global sales arena, cultural intelligence is as crucial as product knowledge. By weaving together a deep understanding of diverse cultures with a genuine respect for their customs and norms, sales professionals can unlock the full potential of global markets.

In closing, let's remember that the world is brimming with opportunities for those willing to reach across cultural lines. The strategies and anecdotes shared here serve as a compass to guide sales professionals in their journey toward becoming adept global sellers, capable of turning the challenges of cross-cultural selling into triumphs of global business success.

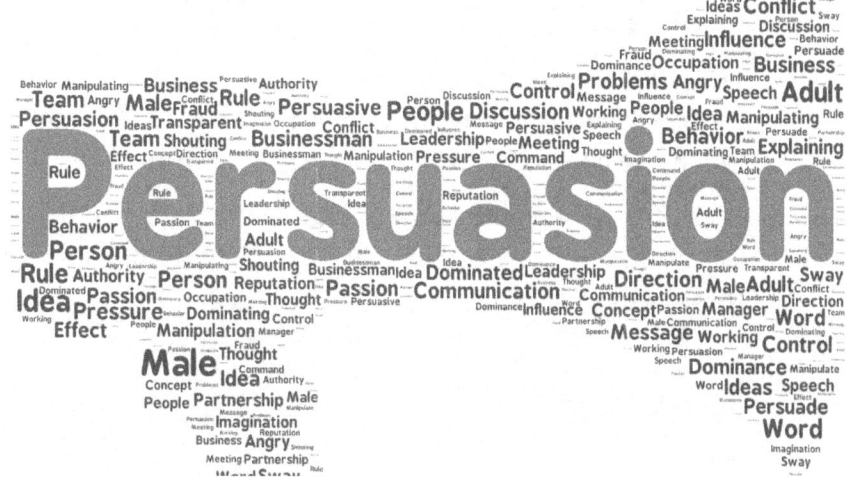

Chapter 36:

Advanced Persuasion Techniques

The Subtleties of Persuasion

Persuasion is an art that combines psychology, timing, and interpersonal skills. This chapter explores nuanced persuasion techniques that can significantly impact the sales process.

Strategic Empathy

- **Strategy Expansion**: Teach sales reps to actively listen and show understanding towards a client's needs and concerns, positioning themselves as a partner rather than just a vendor.

- **Real-Life Example**: A salesperson at Zappos once spent hours on the phone with a customer not just to sell shoes but to form a genuine connection, resulting in the customer becoming a lifelong advocate for the brand.

Narrative Selling

- **Strategy Expansion**: Encourage sales teams to weave product benefits into compelling stories that resonate with the customer's personal or professional life.

- **Case Study**: Apple's success can be partly attributed to its ability to create narratives that frame products as lifestyle enhancements, not just gadgets.

The Contrast Principle

- **Strategy Expansion**: Train reps to present options in such a way that the desired choice appears much more attractive in contrast to the alternatives.

- **Case Study**: Restaurants often use this principle by placing high-priced items near moderately-priced ones, making the latter seem more affordable.

Reciprocity

- **Strategy Expansion**: Instill a culture of giving small, meaningful value-adds to customers without immediate expectation of return, building goodwill and trust.

- **Case Study**: The practice of giving a mint with the bill has been shown in studies to increase tips for waitstaff – a simple act can influence the perception of value.

Social Proof

- **Strategy Expansion**: Utilize testimonials, case studies, and referrals to demonstrate the trust other customers have in the product or service.

- **Case Study**: Dropbox's referral program, which

rewarded both referrer and referee, significantly boosted its user base due to the inherent trust in personal recommendations.

Commitment and Consistency

- **Strategy Expansion**: Help customers make small commitments that steer them towards larger ones, creating a natural progression in the sales funnel.
- **Case Study**: Toyota invites potential customers to configure their dream car online, subtly leading them toward making a purchase decision.

Authority

- **Strategy Expansion**: Establish sales reps as authorities in their field by sharing insights, trends, and data that enrich the customer's understanding of their problems and potential solutions.
- **Case Study**: Salesforce's regular publication of thought leadership pieces has positioned them as experts in the CRM space.

Scarcity

- **Strategy Expansion**: Create urgency by highlighting the exclusivity and limited availability of a product or service.
- **Case Study**: The diamond industry has historically driven demand through the perception of scarcity, despite the abundance of diamonds.

Summary: Key Takeaways

1. Persuasion is more about aligning with customer

needs than pushing a product.

2. Stories that connect products with customers' aspirations can be powerful.

3. Persuasion techniques must be used ethically and with the customer's best interests in mind.

Food for Thought: How can your sales team apply these subtle techniques in a way that is authentic and respects the customer's intelligence and autonomy?

By mastering the subtleties of persuasion, sales teams can improve their ability to connect with clients on a deeper level and facilitate a sales process that feels natural and customer-centric. Integrating these strategies requires a nuanced understanding of human behavior and a commitment to ethical selling practices.

The Principle of Reciprocity

Reciprocity is a powerful motivator in human psychology and, when applied correctly, can be a significant asset in sales. This principle suggests that people feel obliged to return favors or concessions that others make for them.

Reciprocity in Sales Tactics

- **Strategy Expansion**: Train your sales team to offer genuine value upfront without an immediate ask for purchase, building a relationship where the buyer naturally wants to reciprocate.

- **Daily Task**: Encourage sales reps to find opportunities to provide prospects with useful information, assistance, or samples that relate to their interests or needs.

Real-Life Examples and Case Studies

- **Cosmetic Counters**: Makeup brands often provide free makeovers or samples at department store counters. Customers who receive these free services frequently feel compelled to purchase products as a form of reciprocation.

- **Car Dealerships**: Some dealerships offer free car washes or inspections to past customers, who then return when it's time for a new car or for more substantial services, out of a sense of loyalty and reciprocity.

In-Depth Technique Exploration

- **Providing Free Resources**: Sales reps might share a free e-book, guide, or webinar that addresses common customer pain points. HubSpot excels at this, offering a wealth of free resources, which encourages users to consider their paid offerings.

- **Helpfulness without Strings Attached**: A SaaS company could offer free advice or a customized report on industry benchmarks. This positions the sales rep as a trusted advisor, leading to increased sales over time.

Famous Story

- **Ben Franklin Effect**: Benjamin Franklin once asked a rival legislator to lend him a rare book. After the legislator did so, he was much more friendly to Franklin. The favor created a sense of goodwill that improved their relationship. In a sales context, asking for advice or opinions can similarly engage a customer's sense of goodwill.

Daily Training Program

- **Morning Brief**: Each day starts with a briefing on potential value-adding opportunities tailored to specific clients on the day's call list.
- **Role-Playing Scenarios**: Reps practice how to offer value in a way that doesn't come off as manipulative but as genuinely helpful.

Actionable Strategies

1. **Personalization of Favors**: Customize your value offerings to the specific needs or interests of the client to maximize the impact of the reciprocity principle.
2. **Timely Concessions**: Make concessions at strategic points in the negotiation that seem spontaneous and generous, which can often lead to reciprocal concessions from the client.

Food for Thought:

Can you think of a time when you felt compelled to return a favor? How can such natural inclinations be responsibly leveraged in sales?

Summary

The principle of reciprocity can transform transactional interactions into meaningful relationships that foster loyalty and repeated business. Training sales teams to incorporate this principle authentically and respectfully is critical for long-term success.

By integrating these nuanced tactics of reciprocity into your sales team's strategy, you can not only improve immediate sales outcomes but also cultivate a base of repeat customers who value the relationship with your brand and are more likely to advocate on your behalf.

Daily Tasks:

1. **Practice Active Listening**: Work on truly understanding customer needs to tailor your persuasive techniques effectively.

2. **Role Play**: Engage in daily role-play exercises to refine the delivery of persuasive messages.

3. **Reflective Writing**: End each day by journaling about sales interactions to identify what persuasive techniques worked or did not work.

Real-Life Case Study: The Turnaround of Apple

The return of Steve Jobs to Apple in 1997 marked one of the most extraordinary comebacks in business history. By persuasively communicating a vision of innovation and simplicity, Jobs revitalized a struggling brand and repositioned Apple as a leader in technology.

The Contrast Principle

Understanding how the contrast principle can influence decision-making is essential for any sales professional. This psychological phenomenon impacts how we perceive two different things presented one after another. In sales, presenting options in a way that highlights the attractiveness of the primary offer can significantly affect customer choices.

Application of the Contrast Principle in Sales

- **Strategy Expansion**: Teach sales representatives to position premium products or services immediately after presenting a standard option to make the premium choice seem more valuable.

- **Daily Task**: Assign sales reps the exercise of creating contrast scenarios with your product line, focusing on how to present these in real-life customer interactions.

Real-Life Examples and Case Studies

- **Real Estate**: Agents often show a below-average property before showcasing the property they really want to sell. The second house appears much more appealing by contrast, which often persuades buyers to make a higher offer.

- **Retail Clothing**: A store may display high-end items at the front. When customers see the more affordable options afterward, they perceive them as better deals than if they had seen them first.

Famous Story

- **Williams-Sonoma Bread Maker**: Williams-Sonoma introduced an expensive bread maker which almost no one bought. However, when they introduced a slightly higher-end model at a higher price, sales of the first bread maker nearly doubled, illustrating the contrast principle effectively.

Daily Training Program

- **Interactive Learning**: Incorporate daily sessions where sales reps practice sequencing their pitches to leverage contrast effectively.
- **Case Study Reviews**: Have reps review and discuss case studies where the contrast principle has been successfully implemented.

Actionable Strategies

1. **Price Anchoring**: Start with the most expensive option to set a high anchor point. Following options will seem more reasonably priced by contrast.
2. **Feature Comparison**: Create side-by-side comparisons that highlight the benefits of the premium product over the standard option after the standard has been presented.

Food for Thought:

How can we ensure that the use of contrast in sales remains ethical and does not manipulate the customer into making decisions they would not otherwise make?

Summary

The contrast principle is a powerful tool that, when used with integrity, can help customers make more informed decisions while also benefiting the sales team. Mastery of this principle can lead to improved sales metrics and customer satisfaction.

Through careful structuring of options and presentations, sales teams can guide potential buyers to favorable conclusions while maintaining a transparent and customer-focused approach. Integrating the contrast principle with a consultative sales technique can elevate the effectiveness of any sales strategy.

The Scarcity Principle

Scarcity is a powerful driver in human behavior. When we believe something is in limited supply, we want it more. This principle is a staple in sales and marketing strategies because it creates urgency and compels action.

Application of the Scarcity Principle in Sales

- **Strategy Expansion**: Teach sales representatives to communicate the limited availability of products or the time-bound nature of deals to instill a sense of urgency.
- **Daily Task**: Have sales reps identify opportunities in their pipeline where introducing a scarcity element could move a prospect towards a decision.

Real-Life Examples and Case Studies

- **Black Friday Sales**: Major retailers use scarcity by offering "doorbuster" deals that are available in limited quantities, prompting customers to act quickly.
- **Limited Edition Products**: Brands like Apple release limited edition versions of products, which often sell out quickly due to the perceived scarcity.

Famous Story

- **De Beers Diamond Campaign**: De Beers' famous campaign that controlled diamond supply and created an illusion of scarcity transformed diamonds into a symbol of undying love and something to be sought after.

Daily Training Program

- **Scarcity Workshops**: Role-playing exercises where sales reps practice introducing scarcity into sales conversations.

- **Product Knowledge Sessions**: Understanding the inventory and supply chain to accurately communicate scarcity.

Actionable Strategies

1. **Limited-Time Offers**: Create promotions that are only available for a short period, compelling customers to act quickly.

2. **Exclusive Releases**: Introduce products as exclusive or in limited release to increase desirability.

Food for Thought: How can we balance the use of scarcity to drive sales without leading to customer dissatisfaction or brand damage through perceived manipulation?

Summary

The scarcity principle can be a key component in a sales strategy, but it must be used with caution and honesty. It's about creating genuine value and urgency without resorting to deception. By integrating scarcity tactfully, sales teams can elevate the perceived value of their offerings and encourage quicker decision-making from prospects.

By understanding and applying the scarcity principle effectively, sales teams can motivate customers to move forward with purchases they might otherwise delay. This principle, when used ethically, can lead to a win-win situation where customers feel they've made a timely decision, and sales teams achieve their targets.

Training Program:

- **Week 1**: Focus on mastering the principles of persuasion.
- **Week 2-3**: Practice through role-playing different sales scenarios.
- **Week 4**: Review and adapt techniques based on feedback and results.

Actionable Strategies:

- Framing Conversations: Learn to frame conversations in a way that emphasizes the benefits and minimizes the drawbacks.
- Social Proof: Use testimonials and case studies as social proof to bolster your persuasive message.
- Storytelling: Craft compelling stories that connect emotionally with your audience, making your message more memorable and persuasive.

Food for Thought:

- Consider how ethical persuasion differs from manipulation.
- Reflect on the last time you were persuaded. What techniques did the salesperson use?
- How can you ensure that your advanced persuasion

techniques remain customer-centric?

Building a Persuasion Toolkit

Selling isn't just about product knowledge or a smooth pitch; it's about connection, understanding, and influence. This chapter explores the essential components of a "Persuasion Toolkit" and how successful sales professionals employ these tools to engage and convince prospects to make a purchase.

Empathy: The Heart of Understanding

- **Strategy Expansion**: Train sales professionals to practice active listening and to pick up on subtle cues that help them understand the customer's emotional drivers.

- **Daily Task**: Role-playing exercises where sales reps practice responding empathetically to various customer scenarios.

Real-Life Examples and Case Studies

- **Zappos Customer Service**: Zappos empowers its customer service team to use empathy to create memorable customer experiences, which has led to a high customer retention rate.

Rapport Building: The Foundation of Trust

- **Strategy Expansion**: Techniques for mirroring body language, matching tone, and showing genuine interest in the customer's challenges.

- **Daily Task**: Sales reps can work on finding common ground within the first few minutes of every sales call or meeting.

Real-Life Examples and Case Studies

- **Southwest Airlines**: Their staff is known for using humor and personal connections to build rapport with customers, making flights more enjoyable and fostering loyalty.

Authority: The Key to Credibility

- **Strategy Expansion**: Sales professionals should not only understand their product thoroughly but also stay informed about industry trends to position themselves as experts.
- **Daily Task**: Allocate time each week for sales team members to engage in continuous learning about their industry and product enhancements.

Real-Life Examples and Case Studies

- **Apple Store Genius Bar**: The "Geniuses" at Apple stores are trained to not only assist with technical issues but also to educate customers, establishing authority and trust.

Daily Training Program

- **Empathy Training**: Exercises aimed at improving emotional intelligence and customer-centric thinking.
- **Rapport-Building Drills**: Sessions focused on storytelling, active listening, and creating personal connections with clients.
- **Authority Workshops**: Regular updates on product and industry knowledge, as well as training on how to

effectively communicate this expertise.

Actionable Strategies

1. **Customer Persona Development**: Creating detailed customer personas to help sales reps understand and empathize with the target audience.

2. **Trust-Building Activities**: Regular team-based activities that can be translated to customer interactions to build trust quickly.

3. **Expertise Demonstrations**: Regularly creating content, such as blog posts or webinars, where sales reps can showcase their knowledge.

Food for Thought: While building a toolkit of persuasion techniques is vital, it's just as important to maintain a balance between influence and manipulation. How do we define this line, and what measures can we put in place to ensure we remain on the right side of it?

Summary

In this chapter, we emphasize that a well-stocked Persuasion Toolkit is crucial for any sales professional. Empathy allows for genuine connections, rapport building fosters trust, and authority cements credibility. By providing real-life examples and actionable strategies, sales teams can understand and integrate these tools to elevate their sales approach.

Advanced persuasion techniques are the arsenal of the seasoned sales professional. Through strategic application and a deep understanding of human psychology, these methods can dramatically improve sales outcomes. The chapter has explored principles like reciprocity, contrast, and scarcity, supported by daily tasks and a robust training program to ensure these techniques can be honed and applied effectively.

Remember, at the core of all persuasive efforts is the relationship between seller and buyer. As such, trust and genuine interest in the customer's needs remain the bedrock of successful sales strategies.

In conclusion, the art of persuasion, when practiced with integrity and empathy, can lead to not just a sale, but the creation of a long-term, loyal customer relationship. By studying the stories of successful persuaders like Steve Jobs and Oprah Winfrey, and by building and refining your toolkit, you can elevate your sales craft to new heights.

Chapter 37:

Future-proofing Your Sales Career

Introduction

As the world of sales evolves at a breakneck pace, the fear of obsolescence looms large for many professionals. However, with the right approach, you can not only adapt to the future but also become a trailblazer within it. This chapter is dedicated to strategies that will ensure your sales career remains robust and relevant, no matter what changes the future may bring.

The Ever-Evolving Landscape

The digital revolution has fundamentally changed the way we sell, from online marketing to the rise of AI and machine learning. Embracing these changes is not optional; it is essential for survival in the industry.

Real-Life Anecdote: The Evolution of a Sales Giant

Consider the transformation of IBM from a hardware giant to a leader in cloud computing and AI. This shift required not just a change in products but also a change in sales strategy. IBM's sales team had to evolve, learning to sell solutions and outcomes rather than just products.

- **Future-Proof Foundations**

- To ensure longevity in the fast-paced world of sales, teams must build a foundation that not only stands firm in the face of change but also thrives because of it. This chapter outlines how to instill adaptability, technology proficiency, and a value-based selling approach in your team.

- **Adaptability: The Art of Agile Selling**

- **Strategy Expansion**: Encourage a culture where sales teams are comfortable with experimentation and learning from failures. This can involve regular training sessions on new market developments and sales methodologies.

- **Real-Life Example**: IBM has continually evolved over the decades by adapting its sales strategies to align with shifting market demands, from hardware to software, to cloud services.

- **Technology Proficiency: The Modern Salesperson's Arsenal**

- **Strategy Expansion**: Provide ongoing training on the latest CRM software, social media platforms, and sales automation tools. Encourage sales teams to become proficient in using data analytics to tailor their sales approaches.

- **Real-Life Example**: Salesforce continually trains its salesforce in their own and complementary technologies, ensuring that they can fully leverage their CRM's capabilities to optimize their sales processes.

- **Value-Based Selling: The Core of Contemporary Sales**
- **Strategy Expansion**: Shift the focus from selling products or services to selling solutions that address specific customer pain points. This involves a deep understanding of the customer's business and industry.
- **Real-Life Example**: The approach taken by companies like HubSpot, selling inbound marketing as a holistic solution for businesses' growth challenges, has positioned them as a leader in their space.
- **Impact of Specific Technologies and Market Trends**
- **Strategy Expansion**: Keep a close eye on emerging technologies such as AI and machine learning, and anticipate how they could change customer behavior or sales processes.
- **Case Study**: The rise of AI chatbots has revolutionized customer service, with companies like Drift using them to qualify leads before they even reach the sales team.
- **Actionable Exercises and Action Plans**
- **Adaptability Workshops**: Role-play exercises that simulate market shifts, requiring sales teams to adjust their strategies on the fly.
- **Tech Tuesdays**: Weekly sessions dedicated to exploring a new sales technology or platform.
- **Value Mapping Sessions**: Workshops where sales teams map out the customer journey and identify key value propositions at each stage.
- **Summary**

- Building a foundation that's resistant to the winds of change involves fostering adaptability, technology proficiency, and a deep focus on providing value. By training sales teams in these areas and encouraging a proactive rather than reactive approach, sales operations can become truly future-proof.

- **Food for Thought**

- How can your sales team preempt the challenges of tomorrow? What steps can you take today to ensure that your sales strategies are resilient against the inevitable advancements in technology and shifts in market dynamics?

- of the product.

Daily Tasks and Training Program:

1. **Continuous Learning**: Dedicate time each day to learning about new sales tools, techniques, and industry trends.

2. **Soft Skills Development**: Improve your communication, emotional intelligence, and creative problem-solving skills.

3. **Networking**: Build and maintain a network that includes a diverse group of professionals, both within and outside the sales industry.

Case Study: The Salesforce Revolution

Salesforce has consistently stayed ahead of the curve by not only selling CRM solutions but also by predicting and shaping the future of sales itself. They have built a community around their platform, encouraging continuous learning and adaptation among their users.

Actionable Strategies for Dynamic Sales Mastery

In the digital age, the most successful sales teams are those that engage in continuous learning and industry engagement. This chapter explores how leveraging online platforms, connecting with thought leaders, and participating in professional groups can create a proactive and knowledgeable sales force.

Leverage Online Learning Platforms

Online learning platforms provide a wealth of knowledge tailored to various aspects of sales and industry-specific skills.

- **Strategy Expansion**: Encourage sales teams to dedicate time each week to professional development through these platforms. Create a culture where sharing new insights gained from these courses is the norm.

- **Real-Life Example**: Oracle has leveraged platforms like LinkedIn Learning to provide its sales team with up-to-date training on software updates and new sales methodologies, keeping them competitive in a rapidly evolving tech landscape.

Engage with Thought Leaders

Thought leaders can offer valuable insights and foresight into sales trends and strategies.

- **Strategy Expansion**: Create a list of influential sales and industry leaders for your team to follow on platforms like LinkedIn and Twitter. Schedule regular discussions about new insights or strategies these thought leaders are talking about.

- **Real-Life Example**: Sales professionals at HubSpot are

known to engage with thought leaders online, often incorporating cutting-edge sales tactics into their approach, which has contributed to the company's reputation for innovative sales strategies.

Participate in Industry Groups

Being active in industry groups and forums is an excellent way for sales professionals to exchange ideas and stay ahead of emerging trends.

- **Strategy Expansion**: Encourage team members to join and be active in industry-specific LinkedIn groups or forums like Reddit's r/sales. Discuss key takeaways during team meetings.
- **Real-Life Example**: The sales team at Salesforce is an active participant in various CRM and sales strategy groups, allowing them to stay informed and adapt their strategies to best practices and trends.

Impact of Specific Technologies and Market Trends on Sales Strategies

- **Strategy Expansion**: Identify key technologies such as AI, big data, and automation that are shaping sales strategies. Conduct workshops to explore how these can be integrated into your sales process.
- **Case Study**: The adoption of AI for lead scoring by companies like Drift allows sales teams to prioritize their efforts more effectively, focusing on leads that are more likely to convert based on data-driven insights.

Actionable Exercises and Action Plans

1. **Weekly Learning Goals**: Set specific learning targets for each team member and track progress in team

meetings.

2. **Thought Leader Roundtables**: Host monthly virtual roundtable discussions where the team can discuss and debate recent thought leadership pieces.

3. **Industry Immersion Days**: Dedicate one day each quarter to participate in online industry conferences, webinars, and networking events.

Summary

Continuous learning, engagement with thought leaders, and active participation in professional groups are key strategies for sales teams to remain agile and informed. By incorporating these practices, sales professionals can stay at the cutting edge of sales techniques and industry knowledge.

Food for Thought

How can you create a structured yet flexible learning environment within your sales team that encourages curiosity and proactive skill development? What measures can you implement to ensure that this learning translates into actionable sales strategies?

Food for Thought:

- Reflect on how your current skills match up with the direction in which the sales industry is heading.

- How can you cultivate a personal brand that showcases your adaptability and forward-thinking nature?

- Consider what 'future-proof' means in the context of your specific industry and role.

Summary:

Future-proofing your sales career is not a one-time effort; it is an ongoing process of adaptation and growth. By studying the success stories of companies like IBM and Salesforce, you can glean insights into how to remain relevant and successful.

This chapter has laid out a roadmap for staying ahead of the curve, with daily tasks designed to build resilience and adaptability into your professional routine. By fostering a commitment to continuous learning, leveraging technology, and focusing on providing value, you can ensure that your sales career thrives for years to come.

Remember, the future of sales is not just about what you sell or how you sell it, but also about who you are as a sales professional. Cultivating the right mindset and skillset will not only prepare you for the changes ahead but will also position you as a leader in the evolution of the sales industry.

In closing, the journey to future-proofing your sales career begins with a single step: the decision to invest in yourself. With the strategies outlined in this chapter, you are now equipped to take that step with confidence, knowing that you have the tools to navigate and shape the future of sales.

Chapter 38:

Harnessing Technology in Sales

Introduction

In the dynamic world of sales, technology is no longer a luxury—it's a necessity. The modern salesperson must be a hybrid of traditional interpersonal skills and digital savvy. This chapter explores how to harness technology to enhance sales effectiveness, efficiency, and engagement, providing readers with a comprehensive view of today's tech-driven sales landscape.

The Digital Revolution in Sales

The sales landscape has undergone a seismic shift with the advent of digital technology. This chapter examines how technology has revolutionized sales practices and how embracing these changes can lead to unprecedented success.

Technology's Role in Modern Sales

Digital tools have transformed traditional sales processes,

enabling teams to reach and engage customers as never before.

- **Strategy Expansion**: Integrate CRM systems, social selling, email automation, and virtual presentations into the sales process. Utilize analytics to track performance and customer engagement.

- **Real-Life Example**: Salesforce, a leader in cloud-based CRM solutions, uses its own technology to manage customer relationships, demonstrating the power of digital tools in tracking customer interactions and personalizing sales approaches.

Impact of Technologies on Sales Strategies

The right technology can greatly enhance sales strategy, enabling more personalized and efficient customer interactions.

- **Strategy Expansion**: Leverage AI for predictive analytics to forecast sales trends and identify promising leads. Use mobile technology to ensure sales teams have real-time access to data and can respond quickly to customer inquiries.

- **Case Study**: IBM's implementation of Watson, their AI platform, has enabled their sales teams to analyze vast amounts of data to identify customer needs and predict buying patterns.

Digital Prospecting

Digital tools have opened up new avenues for prospecting, from social media platforms to online marketplaces.

- **Strategy Expansion**: Encourage sales reps to use LinkedIn for social selling, engaging with potential leads by sharing relevant content and participating in industry discussions.

- **Real-Life Example**: HubSpot's sales team uses inbound marketing techniques to attract leads online, then engages with them through automated email sequences that nurture these leads down the sales funnel.

Exercises and Action Plans for Sales Teams

1. **CRM Mastery**: Schedule regular CRM training sessions to ensure the sales team can fully utilize all the features available to them.
2. **Social Selling Drills**: Conduct workshops where sales reps create personalized outreach messages based on potential leads' social media activity.
3. **Analytics Interpretation**: Teach sales teams to interpret sales data and analytics to make informed decisions about which leads to pursue.

Summary

The digital revolution has provided sales teams with an array of tools to enhance their processes and strategies. By adopting these technologies, sales professionals can prospect more effectively, engage customers more personally, and close deals more efficiently.

Food for Thought

In an era where technology is at your fingertips, how can you ensure that your sales team is not only equipped with the latest digital tools but also proficient in using them to their full potential?

Strategic Use of Sales Technologies

In the digital age, a savvy sales team's arsenal is powered by technology. From managing leads to closing deals, the strategic use of sales technologies can create efficiencies and provide insights that drive success.

CRM Systems: The Backbone of Sales Management

CRM systems have become the backbone of modern sales management, providing a centralized platform for tracking sales activities and customer interactions.

- **Strategy Expansion**: Implement CRM solutions that align with your sales processes, ensuring that all customer touchpoints are logged and leveraged for future engagement.
- **Real-Life Example**: At Cisco, the use of Salesforce CRM has not only streamlined their global sales process but also enabled them to personalize customer interactions, leading to increased customer satisfaction and sales.

Data Analytics: The Lens for Sales Insight

Data analytics platforms help sales teams to decipher patterns, predict outcomes, and make informed decisions.

- **Strategy Expansion**: Integrate data analytics into your sales strategy to gain a deeper understanding of customer preferences, market trends, and sales performance.
- **Case Study**: Netflix's use of analytics to understand viewer preferences has been key to their content strategy, directly influencing their sales and retention by ensuring they invest in content that has a high likelihood of success.

Social Selling: Building Relationships in the Digital Age

Social selling has redefined how sales professionals connect with prospects, allowing for more meaningful engagement and relationship-building.

- **Strategy Expansion**: Use social selling as a way to establish thought leadership and build trust with potential customers by providing them with value before the sales pitch is ever made.

- **Real-Life Example**: IBM's sales team uses LinkedIn to share insightful content and engage with prospects, positioning themselves as industry experts and trusted advisors, not just salespeople.

Exercises and Action Plans for Sales Teams

1. **CRM Role-Playing**: Engage your team in role-playing exercises that mimic various CRM scenarios, helping them to become proficient in tracking and managing customer interactions.

2. **Analytics Deep Dive**: Conduct workshops where sales reps learn to interpret sales data, identifying key performance indicators that can inform their sales strategies.

3. **Social Selling Challenges**: Create a challenge for sales reps to connect with a certain number of prospects or to generate leads through social media engagement.

Summary

The strategic use of sales technologies can provide a competitive edge, enabling sales teams to manage relationships more effectively, gain valuable insights, and connect with customers in the digital space.

Food for Thought

As sales technologies continue to evolve, how can your team remain agile and adept at adopting new tools? What processes can you establish to ensure technology enhances rather than complicates your sales efforts?

Daily Tasks and Training Program

The day-to-day activities of a sales team are vital in driving the overall success of any sales strategy. Integrating technology, analytics, and social engagement into daily routines ensures that sales professionals are maximizing every opportunity to close deals and build relationships.

CRM Mastery

Understanding the full capabilities of your CRM system can transform the efficiency and effectiveness of a sales team.

- **Strategy Expansion**: Dedicate specific times each day for team members to update all customer interactions in the CRM, ensuring that data is current and actionable.
- **Real-Life Example**: At HubSpot, sales teams spend part of their day not only updating the CRM but also utilizing its insights to tailor their follow-up tasks and personalize customer interactions, leading to higher conversion rates.

Data-Driven Decisions

Making decisions based on sales analytics can significantly improve the accuracy of your sales efforts.

- **Strategy Expansion**: Implement a routine where sales team members review performance dashboards each morning to guide their priorities for the day.

- **Case Study**: Netflix's decision to invest in original content like 'House of Cards' was based on data-driven insights gathered from their subscribers' viewing habits, illustrating the power of analytics in strategic decision-making.

Social Media Engagement

Social media is a powerful tool for sales professionals to connect with prospects and establish themselves as industry thought leaders.

- **Strategy Expansion**: Schedule daily social media activities, including posting industry insights, commenting on trends, and engaging with prospects' content to foster relationships and build credibility.

- **Real-Life Example**: Sales professionals at Adobe regularly engage with content and conversations relevant to their industry on LinkedIn, positioning themselves as valuable resources to their network and increasing their prospecting success.

Exercises and Action Plans for Sales Teams

1. **CRM Drills**: Daily exercises where sales reps practice logging calls, emails, and meetings, and extracting actionable insights from CRM data.

2. **Analytics Interpretation**: Weekly sessions to review sales data trends and develop action plans based on insights.

3. **Social Selling Sprints**: Timed challenges where sales

reps compete to generate leads or build connections via social media engagement.

Summary

The daily integration of CRM mastery, data-driven decision-making, and proactive social media engagement can help sales teams stay agile and responsive to the ever-changing sales landscape.

Food for Thought

How can sales teams balance the need for technological proficiency with the inherently human aspects of sales, such as relationship-building and trust?

Actionable Strategies for Tech-Enabled Sales Efficiency

As technology advances, sales teams need to adapt to stay competitive. This chapter looks at how automation, virtual selling, and mobile enablement can be integrated into sales strategies to increase efficiency and results.

Automate the Routine

Automation can take over repetitive tasks, allowing sales professionals to focus on more complex, value-driven work.

- **Strategy Expansion**: Identify daily, repetitive tasks that can be automated, such as data entry, scheduling meetings, or sending standard follow-up emails.
- **Real-Life Example**: Cisco uses automation to handle routine customer queries, which allows their sales team to focus on more personalized customer interactions and complex problem-solving.

Virtual Selling

Virtual selling has become a mainstay, especially post-pandemic, offering convenience and expanded reach.

- **Strategy Expansion**: Train sales teams on best practices for virtual meetings, including effective use of visuals, engaging presentation skills, and remote rapport-building techniques.

- **Case Study**: SAP embraced virtual selling to maintain and grow their customer relationships when face-to-face meetings were not possible, utilizing virtual tools to demonstrate products and close deals.

Mobile Sales Enablement

Mobile technology provides sales teams with access to information and tools on the go, ensuring they can respond to opportunities and client needs anytime, anywhere.

- **Strategy Expansion**: Equip sales teams with smartphones or tablets loaded with necessary apps and access to the CRM, sales materials, and productivity tools.

- **Real-Life Example**: Salesforce's mobile CRM capabilities allow their sales teams to update and access customer data in real-time, providing them with the agility to respond promptly to leads and customer requests.

Exercises and Action Plans for Sales Teams

1. **Automation Integration**: Have sales reps identify tasks they can automate using their current tools and implement at least one automation per week.

2. **Virtual Selling Role-Play**: Conduct regular training sessions where sales reps practice delivering pitches and handling objections over video conferencing platforms.

3. **Mobile Mastery Challenges**: Set up scenarios where sales reps must use only their mobile devices to complete certain sales tasks, encouraging familiarity and efficiency with mobile tools.

Summary

Incorporating automation, virtual selling, and mobile enablement into sales strategies is not just about keeping up with technology trends; it's about leveraging these tools to make sales processes more efficient and effective.

Food for Thought

- With the array of digital tools available, how can sales teams prioritize which technologies to integrate into their strategies, and how can they ensure these tools are used to their full potential?

- How can you balance the efficiency of technology with the personal touch that sales require?

- Reflect on how customer data collected through technology can be used ethically and effectively.

- Consider the future of sales technology. What emerging tools could revolutionize the way you sell?

Harnessing AI: The Salesforce Einstein Example

Salesforce Einstein is an example of how artificial intelligence is being integrated into CRM to provide predictive analytics, intelligent automation, and personalized customer experiences.

It demonstrates the potential of AI to enhance the sales process at every stage.

Building a Technology-Enhanced Sales Strategy

Today's sales environment demands not just familiarity with technology but a strategy that seamlessly integrates it to enhance every step of the sales process. This chapter provides a roadmap for incorporating technology in ways that amplify sales capabilities and focus on delivering superior customer experiences.

Training and Adaptation for Sales Teams

Ensuring that sales teams are proficient with new technologies is crucial for leveraging their benefits.

- **Strategy Expansion**: Develop a continuous learning environment with scheduled training sessions on new sales tools. Use a mix of e-learning, workshops, and webinars to cater to different learning styles.

- **Real-Life Example**: Dell Technologies has a robust training program for its salesforce that includes both self-paced online courses and instructor-led workshops, ensuring that their team is adept at using the latest sales tools.

Customer-Centric Technology Implementation

Technology should be used to not only make sales processes more efficient but also to enhance the customer buying experience.

- **Strategy Expansion**: Implement CRM systems with customer portals that allow for easy tracking and management of orders, service requests, and communication.

- **Case Study**: Amazon's use of AI to provide personalized recommendations has revolutionized the retail experience, making it easy for customers to find products they're likely to purchase.

Staying Updated on Sales Tech and Trends

To remain competitive, sales teams must keep up with the rapid evolution of sales technology.

- **Strategy Expansion**: Regularly review and assess the latest sales tools and platforms. Consider their applicability to your business and the potential benefits they could bring.

- **Real-Life Example**: Adobe stays ahead of the curve by not only developing cutting-edge software but also by adopting the latest sales technologies, such as virtual reality for product demos.

Exercises and Action Plans for Sales Teams

1. **Tech Tuesdays**: Dedicate time each week for the team to learn about a new technology or feature.

2. **Customer Journey Mapping**: Use workshops to map out how technology touches each part of the customer journey and identify areas for improvement.

3. **Tech Trend Reports**: Assign team members to research and present on new sales tech trends, fostering a culture of continuous learning and innovation.

Food for Thought

As you contemplate the integration of new technologies, how will you ensure that these tools are enhancing and not complicating your sales process? What measures will you take to keep your team's skills sharp in an ever-evolving tech landscape?

Summary

Integrating technology into your sales strategy is about more than just staying current; it's about creating a symbiotic relationship between your sales processes and the tools at your disposal to maximize efficiency and enhance the customer experience.

Harnessing technology in sales is about more than just staying current; it's about using digital tools to create a competitive advantage. From Alex's transformation into a top-performing sales rep to Zappos' industry-leading customer service, technology, when used strategically, can lead to unprecedented success.

This chapter has laid out a roadmap for integrating technology into your sales processes, with actionable strategies and daily tasks designed to make technology work for you. By staying informed and adaptable, sales professionals can not only meet the challenges of the digital age but thrive within it.

In closing, as we look to the future of sales, it's clear that technology will continue to play a pivotal role. Whether through AI, CRM, or social selling, the ability to leverage these tools will define the next generation of sales leaders. With the insights and strategies provided in this chapter, you are well-equipped to be at the forefront of this technological evolution in sales.

Chapter 39:

Health and Well-Being for Sales

Introduction

In the high-stakes arena of sales, success is often measured by numbers and achievements. However, an essential, yet frequently overlooked component is the health and well-being of the sales professional. Long hours, high pressure, and the constant pursuit of targets can take a toll. This chapter is devoted to the well-being of those in the trenches of sales, providing a comprehensive guide to maintaining physical health, mental clarity, and emotional resilience.

The Vitality of the Sales Force

A healthy salesperson is a successful salesperson. Just as a finely-tuned engine powers a car to victory, a well-cared-for body and mind propel a sales professional to peak performance. We'll explore strategies for sustaining high energy levels, sharp mental focus, and a positive mindset.

Real-Life Anecdote: The Marathoner's Mindset

Meet Lisa, a veteran sales director whose marathon training became a metaphor for her sales approach. She learned that rest, proper nutrition, and pacing—principles crucial to endurance running—were equally vital to her sales performance and longevity in her career.

Case Study: A Corporate Shift in Well-Being

Google's well-known wellness programs exemplify a corporate acknowledgment of the importance of employee health. By offering resources for physical health, mental wellness, and even napping pods, Google has set a precedent for how supporting well-being can lead to increased productivity and job satisfaction.

The Pillars of Health in Sales

- **Physical Health**: Regular exercise, adequate sleep, and proper nutrition are non-negotiable for sustaining the energy that sales demands.
- **Mental Health**: Mindfulness practices, time management, and regular breaks can prevent burnout and maintain mental sharpness.
- **Emotional Health**: Building supportive relationships, work-life balance, and pursuing hobbies can enhance emotional resilience.

Daily Tasks and Training Program:

1. **Exercise Routine**: Encourage a daily physical activity regimen tailored to individual preferences and schedules.

2. **Mindfulness Practice**: Integrate short mindfulness exercises or meditation into the daily routine to reduce stress and enhance focus.

3. **Nutritional Planning**: Provide training on nutrition and its impact on performance, and encourage planning healthy meals.

Actionable Strategies:

- **Ergonomic Workspaces**: Invest in creating a sales environment that supports physical health, including standing desks and ergonomic chairs.

- **Mental Health Days**: Advocate for mental health days off, allowing sales professionals to recharge when needed.

- **Emotional Intelligence Training**: Offer workshops on developing emotional intelligence to navigate the stresses of sales effectively.

Food for Thought:

- How does your current lifestyle support or hinder your sales performance?

- In what ways can you integrate well-being into your daily sales routine without compromising productivity?

- Reflect on the connection between your physical, mental, and emotional health and your ability to sell.

Personal Stories: The Resilient Sales Leaders

Sales leaders like Arianna Huffington and Richard Branson emphasize well-being as a cornerstone of success. After experiencing exhaustion, Huffington became an advocate for sleep and wellness, while Branson credits his fitness routine as a key factor in his business achievements.

Creating a Balanced Sales Life

Balancing the demands of sales with personal health requires:

- **Strategic Rest**: Understanding that rest is not idleness, but a strategic tool for long-term performance.

- **Wellness Culture**: Fostering a team culture that values health and well-being.

- **Continuous Learning**: Staying informed about the latest research and trends in health and wellness.

Summary:

This chapter has underscored the integral role health and well-being play in the life of a sales professional. From the daily discipline of exercise and nutrition to the corporate wellness initiatives of companies like Google, the focus on well-being is proving to be a key differentiator in sales success.

By adopting the strategies outlined here, sales professionals can enhance their quality of life and, in turn, their sales performance. The anecdotes and case studies demonstrate that when companies invest in the well-being of their employees, the return on investment is reflected in a more motivated, productive, and successful sales force.

In closing, the health and well-being of sales professionals should not be an afterthought but a foundational element of sales strategy. As the stories of leaders like Huffington and Branson illustrate, prioritizing well-being is not just good for the individual but also good for business. By embracing the principles of a balanced, health-conscious sales lifestyle, professionals can ensure that their success is sustainable and that they are selling not just quickly, but wisely and well.

Thank you for reading !!

PS.If you enjoyed reading this book, please leave an honest review. This helps other readers find the book they need ★★★★★

www.ingramcontent.com/pod-product-compliance
Lightning Source LLC
Chambersburg PA
CBHW072143290526
45794CB00004B/1400